Praise for The Rebus Guide to Publishing Open Textbooks (So Far)

"Rebus is a godsend! I rely heavily on their amazing guides and templates; it's a thorough and thoughtful approach to creating open textbooks that both makes the process easier, and the end product better."

— Allison Brown, Digital Publishing Services Manager, SUNY Geneseo

"The Rebus guide is required reading for OER projects big and small. It helped me organize my textbook project for grant applications and anticipate potential issues on a large multi-site team. I owe the plaudits I get for organization to Rebus for creating such an accessible and practical resource!"

— Matt DeCarlo, Assistant Professor of Social Work, Radford University

"The Rebus guide is an invaluable resource that has helped me plan publishing projects within my organization. It includes document templates, links to additional resources, and great advice that save time and ensure a thoughtful approach. I'd recommend this guide for anyone looking to gain valuable insight on developing open texts."

— Alisa Lazear, Community & Content Manager, Canadian Legal Information Institute

The Rebus Guide to Publishing Open Textbooks (So Far)

The Rebus Guide to Publishing Open Textbooks (So Far)

APURVA ASHOK AND ZOE WAKE HYDE

Rebus Community

Montréal

4 Steps to Starting an Open Textbook Project

No matter the stage of your project, a Rebus Community homepage is a place to build your team, discuss your book's progress, and attract potential supporters. To get yours, follow these steps:

1. Start your project at www.rebus.community.
2. Click "Create a Project"
3. Tell us about your book, team, audience, subject, and license.
4. Use *The Rebus Guide to Publishing Open Textbooks (So Far)* to create your book.

If you have any questions, we're here to help. Ask the community at www.rebus.community/c/help-questions.

About Rebus Community

The Rebus Guide to Publishing Open Textbooks (So Far) was produced by the Rebus Community, an initiative of the Rebus Foundation.

Rebus Community is a non-profit organization that helps educational institutions build human capacity in OER publishing through professional development. We offer both in-depth courses and webinar series for faculty, librarians, and institutional leaders. Our programs demystify open publishing, encourage OER adoption, support faculty to author new content, and introduce students to affordable, high-quality materials. Programs are designed to connect participants to a global OER community.

Join us and learn more at www.rebus.community.

Contents

Acknowledgements

This book is a culmination of more than two years of collaboration, innumerable conversations and exchanges, and a wide range of collective knowledge and experience. We are extremely grateful to everyone in the Rebus Community who worked with us to learn the ins-and-outs of OER publishing and let us be a part of their open textbook projects. We appreciate your willingness to trial new methods and models, and for your support and encouragement as we began creating the guide to capture what we learned. None of this would be possible without you!

In particular, we'd like to thank the following project leads, and all those involved in their teams:

- Adriano Palma
- Allison Brown
- Amanda Taintor
- Andre Mount
- Ann Ludbrook
- Arthur Gill Green
- Beau Branson
- Benjamin Martin
- Billy Meinke-Lau
- Brian Barnett
- Carrie Cuttler
- Cathie LeBlanc
- Chelsea Green
- Christina Hendricks
- Danielle Mead Skjelver
- Dave Braunschweig
- Dave Dillon
- Deborah Amory
- Douglas Giles
- Eran Asoulin
- George Matthews
- Heather Exner-Pirot

- Heather Salazar
- Jennifer Paris
- Jessica Kirchner
- Julie Ward
- Justin Marlowe
- Katie Kirakosian
- Linda Frederiksen
- Liz Mays
- Luis R. Izquierdo
- Maha Bali
- Mark Poepsel
- Michelle Ferrier
- Michelle Schwartz
- Michelle Reed
- Nadine Aboulmagd
- Naomi Wahls
- Paul Hackett
- Rajiv Jhangiani
- Ryan Hersha
- Sarah Hare
- Scott Clifton
- Sharon Kioko
- Stan Yu
- Susan Jones
- Timothy Robbins
- Valery Vinogradovs
- Werner Westermann

There are a few more people whose involvement we must acknowledge: David Szanto, your sharp editor's eyes and pattern-spotting, connections-making abilities were invaluable to making this book more cohesive. Thanks also for your work directing and editing the video series version of the guide, so it's available in yet another format for others to discover and use. Mei Lin, thank you for creating transcripts and captions for the video series and making sure they are more accessible. Liz Mays, your early efforts towards the guide back in 2018 got us started, and we're grateful that you come back to contribute your expertise in our sections on editing and marketing. Billy Meinke-Lau; Jess Mitchell and the team at IDRC; Lauri Aesoph, Josie Gray, and the team at BCcampus Open Education; Deb Quentel — thanks for letting us pick your brains, build on your work, and use your tools as we put this guide together.

Thanks to Hugh McGuire for painting the big picture of how open tools, process, and books can change the world — it motivated us to continue taking small steps and contribute what we can towards that future. And speaking of open tools, thank you to the team at Pressbooks for creating the software that lets us easily create and share this collective knowledge with the widest possible audience!

Finally, thank you to all the readers and users of this guide — for giving it a go and for letting this book become part of your universe, and in so doing, for becoming part of its community!

Introduction

From the beginning, the Rebus Community as an organization has been dedicated to building a new, collaborative model for open textbook creation in partnership with the OER community. Our idea of this model has also always been that it be *replicable* and *scalable*, meaning that anyone – including you, the undoubtedly intrepid OER creator reading this guide – should be able to use it to create and adapt more and more OER without running into the limitations of traditional publishing models. From early on, we knew we had to think hard about how to actually go about achieving this vision — not only how we would develop our model and share it with the world, but also how it could then continue to grow and change over time as the community needs and values evolve.

There's no one way to meet that goal, but this guide, and how we went about creating it, is one of them. It is the result of thousands of hours of work by dozens of open textbook creators who were generous enough to allow us to join forces and learn about open textbook publishing together. We have spent many months researching, creating resources, problem solving, celebrating, commiserating, and more with the projects we've supported – all the while being responsive to their needs and learning not just from them, but also from the wider OER community.

This guide is our effort to distill that learning and experience into a comprehensively documented process for you to use, in part or in whole, keeping as true to or deviating as much from it as you choose. While it does a deep dive into the publishing process, it also includes summaries and videos for each section to give you an easier pathway in. In addition, the templates and examples throughout keep it grounded very much in the practical. This is a useful book. It's made to be used. It's also made to be used in whatever way is useful to you, whether that means reading it start to finish, out of order, in pieces, skimming quickly, or any other way you can find.

We've also worked hard to make it easy to tackle big questions like how to make sure your content is accessible, and how to manage a big team of volunteer contributors. Our philosophy of creation as a collaborative act is woven throughout, as is the belief we share with the community that OER content should be created to serve all students, with all their unique contexts, understandings of the world, needs, and goals.

The goal of this guide is very simply to help you create quality OER, build a community around it, and have it make a positive impact in the world. We believe that those in the classroom – both instructors and students – know best what they need to be successful in their teaching and learning. What they and those supporting them on campuses (librarians, instructional designers, etc.) don't always know is how to go about creating and publishing their content. To do so, they have typically had to invent a process, or pull together information from many sources. But, true to the open education ethos, there is no need to reinvent the wheel!

This guide offers concrete, practical steps to go from the idea of a textbook (or other OER) to a thriving community gathered around a robust resource being used in classrooms around the world. It's also just as useful if you want to work with a small team on a resource for your own classroom, that may or may not end up being used by others. At every stage, you get to decide what works best for you. Whether you're a faculty member acting as lead author or editor, or a librarian or OER program manager tasked with supporting creation on your campus, we've got you covered.

The final critical piece of this guide is the fact that it is a living document, and will continue to change and improve over time. This is reflected in the title, of course, and we very much want the community at large to be part of the evolution. So, if you've read or used this guide and have some thoughts – maybe something worked well or not, maybe you came up with another approach, maybe there's something missing, or something is overly-complicated – please share them with us on the Rebus Community project home. We also encourage you to share this resource with anyone you know who is starting out on their OER creation journey, or who is looking to add some more tools to their belt.

The Rebus Community has never sought to be the gatekeepers of knowledge. We don't want to keep it for ourselves and dole it out to a select few as we see fit. Knowledge shouldn't be contained, and knowledge should never come from only one source. These principles inform the very best of what open education has to offer, and we take them very seriously. This guide is a prime example of that philosophy, and we hope it serves you well on your adventures.

BUILDING A TEAM

Building a Team Summary

The idea that books are the work of a single person, the author, is a bit of a myth, really. In reality, it takes a village to create any book. Even single-author or self-published book will have editors, proofreaders, designers, and ultimately, readers who come to form a community around the book. Creating, publishing, and sharing knowledge is not a solo endeavour!

This section will cover what to keep in mind as you're building and managing a team as part of your open textbook project.

<table>
<tr><td>Underlying principles</td></tr>
<tr><td>

Teams come in all shapes and sizes. Whether you're a team of four or forty, it's important to have people who are invested in the project, and believe in its mission and goals.

It's not just about sharing the workload. Having a diverse and representative mix of people on your project lets different perspectives and experiences shape the book, so it's not just a product of one person and actually reflects the experiences of readers.

Communication is the key to a well-functioning team. Set up clear expectations about what needs doing, and be sure to communicate clearly and frequently with your team to avoid delays and surprises.

Every team needs project champions or cheerleaders. Reminding your team about successes along the way, and having someone cheering them on at each step does wonders for team morale. Not only will this lift spirits, but

</td></tr>
</table>

may even encourage team members to do more for the project by adopting or marketing the book.

Who's Involved?

As you start to put your team together, make sure you think about the many combinations of people you can ask to be involved. We've often seen OER and open textbooks projects include:

- Project leaders
- Contributors at all scales
- Students (graduate and undergraduate)
- Advisors
- OER champions or advocates
- Institutional supporters, eg.: instructional designers, librarians, accessibility experts, etc.
- Interested observers

Key Tactics

If you're leading a team, here are some things you should keep in mind to nurture your team, so it grows into a thriving community of practice around your book:

- Recognize the efforts of each contributor, big or small, that goes into making the resource what it is.
- Develop community guidelines to create a safe environment for your team (and make sure people follow them!).
- Sign MOUs, contracts, or other agreements so expectations are clear.

> • Make sure clear documentation on the project goals, roles and responsibilities is available to all team members and kept up to date.
>
> • Set an example for your team, so they can look up to you and emulate your behaviour over the course of the project.
>
> • Be kind and understanding – everyone is juggling responsibilities and we're all only human!

Ultimately, having a team around the book ensures that the project will be an easier and more enjoyable experience, and that the resource will be more valuable and valued – so try to make your project a social, collaborative, and overall fun experience!

Read on to explore the whys and hows of building a team for your open textbook project.

Building a Team Overview

This section of *The Rebus Guide to Publishing Open Textbooks (So Far)* will help you understand why teams are important, what makes a good team, how you can recruit new members to join your project, and more. It is licensed under a Creative Commons Attribution 4.0 International License (CC BY) and you are welcome to print this document, make a copy for yourself, or share with others.

If you're looking to build a team around an open textbook project, or not sure why this is necessary, read through the sections below, and consider the suggestions as you get started.

If you have any questions about this, or any other of our guides, please feel free to post them in the Rebus Community project home. This document is an evolving draft, based on our experience managing open textbook projects and community feedback. We welcome your thoughts and contributions, so let us know how it works for you, or if you have any suggestions to improve the guide.

LET'S START WITH SOME MYTHBUSTING

There's a fairly common, persistent (and completely untrue) idea around books that they are the work of a single person: the author. By having the author's name plastered on the cover, their photo everywhere, and the long cultural history of authors and their solitary, tortured genius, the reality of what it takes to publish a book is obscured. But make no mistake – it takes a village.

The same is true with academic and educational publishing, where the focus is typically on the author or a small team of authors and their contributions. However, no book has ever been the work of just one person. Even single-author or self-published books will have editors, proofreaders, designers, and ultimately, readers who come to form a community around the book. Creating, publishing, and sharing knowledge is **not a solo endeavour**.

Knowing, then, that making (and reading) a textbook is a collective effort, start thinking early on about who you want to have involved in your project, what they bring to the table, and what they can get from being a part of the team.

WHY IS HAVING A TEAM IMPORTANT?

Teams bring a number of benefits to a project, and open up the potential for you and your resource to have an even bigger impact than if it were just you chipping away at the book.

A team around your textbook ensures that you have:

- people to help share the workload
- different perspectives and experiences that feed into the creation of the book
- varying areas of subject expertise and knowledge
- the option to draw on others' time, skills, and expertise as the need arises
- built-in networking
- built-in marketing for the book
- a pool of potential adopters
- others invested in the long-term maintenance of the book
- an enjoyable, social, collaborative, and overall fun experience!

Research shows that a *diverse* team encourages innovation, creativity, thinking, and can help you create a resource with a wider reach. For instance, diverse teams can help ensure that the book's content is reflective of the world that learners inhabit, can help develop exercises or examples where all students can see themselves, and ultimately see to it that the resource does not reinforce the status quo or perpetuate stereotypes. A team that includes not just subject matter experts, but also instructors who have taught or will be teaching with the resource, can also make certain that the resource has a practical value in classrooms and to students.

WHAT MAKES A TEAM?

Teams come in many combinations, but all begin with...you! Your contribution and participation in the project is invaluable, regardless of whether you are the project leader or volunteer on a small task.

In our experience, teams around open textbook or OER projects often also include:

- Project leaders
- Contributors at all scales, be it a person writing five chapters, or someone proofreading just one
- Students (graduate and undergraduate)
- Advisors or some form of wise counsel
- OER champions or advocates
- Institutional supporters, such as instructional designers, OER librarians, CLT staff, etc.
- Interested observers
- Potential adopters
- Community members

Teams behind open textbooks aren't just a homogenous group of people with the same experience or role. And this is for the better! See our chapter on roles and responsibilities for a full list of the various team members you might need on your project.

WHAT MAKES A GOOD TEAM?

Good teams don't always form naturally, but often need to be carefully cultivated and looked after! A team is a living, breathing, group of people who need communication, time, attention, and shared understanding to keep working efficiently and happily. We hope these tips will help you cultivate an engaged group of people around your project.

1. Make sure that your team consists of **people who are invested in the project, and believe in its mission and goals**. Your onboarding process for each team member should include a summary of the project's purpose and if possible, a few emphatic sentences from you about why you are involved or what drives you about the project.

2. Encourage members to be **upfront about their workload**, and what they can (and cannot) commit to. With open textbook projects, which are mainly volunteer-driven, there is often no shortage of tasks to complete. You don't want to overburden your team, cause burn-out, or any ill-feelings towards the project.

3. Make sure everyone understands the expectations of a given task when they take it on – you want to be sure that **people complete what they have agreed to work on**. A good team consists of everyone checking off their list of duties, no matter how large or small.

4. **Communication** is integral to a team's performance. Work on creating an atmosphere that encourages team members to talk to one another, share their progress on tasks, and indicate if they require more time or assistance, etc. The more interactions your team members have with each other, the less isolated they will feel, and the stronger the community around the textbook becomes.

5. Each team needs a leader, but with open textbook projects, teams **need more than formal leadership**. As opposed to someone who is just shooting off commands or assigning tasks, open textbooks require **project champions** who will motivate

and update the team, and in so doing, push the project forward. When you find these people, do everything you can to keep them!

6. With a wide group, it can seem difficult to help everyone get along and complete their work, but the key is to make sure that **each person on the team feels valued**, feels like they belong, and are satisfied with their contribution to the project.

7. Good teams ought also have a **mix of people** involved, and should be **representative** of the people who will be using the content. This diversity will help shape the resource through different lenses and perspectives, making it more applicable and useful to a range of users.

8. If the content you're working on involves traditionally marginalized communities, make sure you have representatives from those communities involved from the beginning – always remember, **"nothing about us without us."**

9. No two teams will be the same, and neither should their **measures of success**. A good team will define the intended outcomes of the project together, setting realistic goals for the group and for individuals based on the resources at hand. A team of five people might not be able to take on as much as a team of fifty, but that's okay! Celebrate each completed task and milestone, and think of it as taking your team closer to the final goal.

Now that you know what makes a good team, you can begin putting this group together. Take a look at our recruitment guide to see how to find and onboard new members to your project.

WHAT ARE YOUR RESPONSIBILITIES TO YOUR TEAM AS A LEADER?

Good teams need nurturing and there are a few things that you should do to be a better project lead. This might go without saying, but **be nice** to everyone volunteering their time and energy! While you ought to remain focused about the project and its goals, you should also constantly remember that everyone on the team is only human. The **well-being of the people** on the team is just as important as the project itself, so **be understanding** when things don't go as planned. **Assume the best in people**, as you might not always know what it going on with them or their lives outside of the project.

Part of being a good team player, and a better manager/lead, is also as simple as saying hello to anyone new to the team, and introducing them to the rest of the group! Small things like being welcoming, or publicly thanking people for their contributions show that you **recognise the effort of each contributor**. For more tips, take a look at our volunteer management guide (coming soon!).

If possible, you may want to develop **team or community guidelines** that you can share with each new member that lay out these simple expectations. In addition, as the lead you should **set an example** for the team, and **stick to your deadlines** for any task that you have committed to doing. It's important that you do your portion of the work, or **give enough warning** to your teammates if you can't complete it on time – and be clear that the same is expected of everyone on the team.

An effective way to finalise tasks, deadlines, and expected outcomes or deliverables from your team members is to **sign a contributor MOU, contract, or agreement**. This document can help you clearly summarise your project and its goals, as well as the responsibilities and expectations of each collaborator. You're welcome to use or adapt from our contributor MOU template, or can write your own.

Ultimately, having a team around the book ensures that the project will be an easier and more enjoyable experience, and that the resource will be more valuable and valued! Continue on to the rest of this section to see how best to form this team, manage volunteers, and keep everyone motivated and engaged.

NEED FURTHER ASSISTANCE?

We hope these suggestions will help you build a strong and vibrant community around your project. We'll continue to add to this guide as we work with more projects, and we welcome your ideas on what else we could add, or your feedback on how these approaches have worked (or not!) for you.

If you have questions, or anything to add, please let us know in the Rebus Community project home.

 *This work is licensed under the Creative Commons Attribution 4.0 International License.*

How to Build a Leadership Team

This section of *The Rebus Guide to Publishing Open Textbooks (So Far)* is meant to help you understand the importance of leadership, admin and advisory teams, share suggestions for forming these teams, and more. It is licensed under a Creative Commons Attribution 4.0 International License (CC BY) and you are welcome to print this document, make a copy for yourself, or share with others.

Please read through the sections below, and consider the suggestions as you begin planning your project and setting out with the initial steps. If you have any questions, please feel free to post them in the Rebus Community project home. This document is an evolving draft, based on our experience managing open textbook projects and community feedback. We welcome your thoughts and contributions, so let us know how it works for you, or if you have any suggestions to improve the guide.

WHY IS IT IMPORTANT TO HAVE A LEADERSHIP TEAM?

Seeing an open textbook project through from conception to release is no easy task, especially if you are working as the solo project manager, coordinator, or lead. But, with a good leadership team, you can **share the load and responsibilities**. The right team will make all the difference – helping drive the project forward and ensuring that it runs smoothly.

Having a group of people at the core who are working together to plan, lead, and see a project through to completion also allows you to draw on a **range of perspectives and expertise**. Each individual is unique and comes to a project with their own lens, background, and skills. These powers combined can strengthen your project, make the resource more accessible, and make the collaborative experience more inclusive.

Through providing input from people with varying perspectives and skills, the leadership team can also help with **complex decisions** that arise along the way. They can act as a kind of governing body, committed to helping the resource become as valuable as possible.

This group also lets you expand your network, meaning you have a wider reach when recruiting collaborators, and promoting your book in the long term. And, as an added bonus, it allows you to meet different people passionate about working in Open Education and improving the resources available in your field! As with any collaborative project, an open textbook is an opportunity for you to grow your community and learn more through shared work.

WHAT DOES THE LEADERSHIP TEAM DO?

There are several different approaches you can take to leading a project, and **not everyone has to sign up for a big workload**. One approach is to have both an **admin team** that focuses on the project's day-to-day activities, and an **advisory team** to help steer the project in the right direction as needed.

The admin team can be charged with the **day-to-day managing** of contributors, tasks, deadlines and other project work, working together to keep things moving forward steadily. Typically, admins will also be contributing to the project in other major ways (as an author, editor, or filling in other gaps like formatting, arranging print on demand, etc.).

In contrast, an advisory team (a.k.a. steering committee, brains trust, etc.), can be established to **guide the process at a high level**. This team can set the 'big picture' goals for the project, or measures of success. They can assist with decision-making, mediate conflict, and provide wise counsel as needed. This group should ideally be proactive, rather than reactive, in the face of challenges, and so will rely on the admin team to keep them up to date on what's happening. And, while they might not be involved in the day-to-day, advisors are still a great channel to promote your project and find new contributors!

While it may not be possible for every project to have both of these teams, keep in mind the roles they play as you bring together your project leads and make sure you have a mix of people with different responsibilities in a way that works for you.

SPECIFIC DUTIES AND EXPECTATIONS

As with any collaborative project, it's good to clearly state the duties, responsibilities, or expectations for each team member. Doing so can help to avoid confusion or conflict down the line, and keep everyone on the same page. While not exhaustive, the following lists should give an idea of what the two teams might be responsible for.

Admin team:

- Defining the project
- Preparing project-related documents such as guides, templates, calls, etc.
- Managing the project's public listing on the Rebus Community platform
- Sharing calls for various contributors
- Talking to potential volunteers and onboarding those who are selected
- Tracking content and the project's progress
- Reaching out to people and sending regular reminders
- Engaging with the team
- Conducting a developmental edit on the content
- Reading the resource before it is released

- Acting as a backstop for others on the team
- Clarifying roles and tasks for team members
- Running conference calls with authors or other volunteers

Advisory team:

- Providing input on the project's definition and direction, and the content
- Setting broad strategic objectives for the resource
- Making sure that these goals are met
- Ensuring the team includes diverse perspectives, which are also represented in the content created
- Mediating conflict
- Acting as an impartial body and advising the admin team on decisions
- Helping find and recruit volunteers
- Attending meetings or calls
- Promoting the project from conception to publication

Finally, make sure you discuss any other expectations with the whole leadership team, and spend some time considering decision-making strategies that you can employ over the course of the project. You could also sign a Memorandum of Understanding (MOU) with each member of your team to be certain that you are on the same page regarding their position in the project. We've prepared a template that you could use, or adapt.

RECRUITING MEMBERS FOR BOTH TEAMS

Thinking about the different roles, you can also consider who is best placed to help lead the project, and what expertise they can bring.

The admin team will likely have more of a direct impact on the content, and need to be committed to being hands-on with the project. Experience with open textbook publishing is a plus, and you'll be working closely with them, so they need to be reliable! Here are some of the kinds of people who might be involved:

1. Librarians interested in/in charge of developing OER at your institution

2. Instructional designers or others from your institution's Center for Teaching & Learning

3. Colleagues or graduate students in your department

4. Collaborators on other projects from outside your institution

5. Authors or editors already attached to the project

In addition, when it comes to the advisory team, think about:

1. Senior experts in your field or mentors

2. Anyone you know with experience publishing textbooks or open textbooks

3. Community advisors (this is crucial is you are working with a specific community or with indigenous knowledge)

4. Subject librarians

5. Instructors with experience teaching the course for which the resource is intended

Another thing to consider when forming both teams is whether they are **diverse and representative of the professionals in your field**. This might mean looking outside your existing network, and considering people who might not otherwise be considered for this kind of project (e.g. graduate students).

In addition, including **instructors with experience teaching the course** you are working with means you are more likely to compile a resource with practical value in the classroom. Look for members who have **expertise in the subject**, are **organized**, **committed**, and **buy-in to** the reasons for creating an open resource. It's also important to consider people's **time**

commitments, as being part of the admin team can be a lot of work. If they aren't able to commit, an advisory role might be more suitable.

You might also be wondering **how many people you will need**. Unfortunately, there's no secret formula – it really depends on the project! You should aim for enough members that no one person is left doing all the work, but not so many that no one is clear on who is doing what. And no matter how many individuals you end up recruiting, it is important for them to have a clear understanding of their responsibilities.

Our recruitment guide lists the strategies you can employ to find your team, so have a look through it when you're ready to start looking for people.

EXAMPLES OF LEADERSHIP AND ADVISORY TEAMS IN ACTION

As we mentioned in the introduction, this guide has been developed based on our experiences working with many different open textbook projects around the world. Given that experience, we wanted to share some examples of both leadership and advisory teams in action, so you could better understand their role and importance in the open textbook publishing process.

One of our pilot open textbook projects, *From the Ground Up: An Introduction to North American Archaeology*, set up an advisory team from very early on. The book itself sets out to offer a broad overview of the diverse groups that have called "North America" home for over 10,000 years and how lessons from the past are relevant today. The advisory team comprises a number of subject experts from various kinds of institutions. The project lead, Katie Kirakosian, explains its purpose:

> The Steering Committee was formed to help guide the larger process for creating this open textbook. This Committee will be following the progress of each component of this project and preparing for upcoming milestones (i.e. sending out sections for review, marketing the textbook, etc). Steering Committee members may be asked to

offer their advice if/when issues arise that need to be discussed by an impartial group that knows the landscape of North American Archaeology quite well. The goal is for the Steering Committee to be proactive versus reactionary in this progress by focusing on addressing the complex and varied needs and potential challenges during the life of this project. **If you have a concern arise while working on this project, email Katie Kirakosian directly who can offer advice or bring the concern to the attention of the Steering Committee, if necessary. Please do not email the Steering Committee directly!**

Another pilot project, *Introduction to Philosophy*, needed a large, dedicated admin team due to the sheer size of the resource being created. The project aimed to create a series of open introductory texts, each in a different sub-field of philosophy. To wrangle a project of this size, each individual text has its own editor, with a series editor overseeing the whole operation. As of writing, the team comprises nine people, located across North America, Europe, and Africa, with two other slots to be filled in future for the remaining sub-fields. While each editor is responsible for the content and contributors in their own portion of the series, they also collectively make decisions about editing and review processes, write or provide feedback on guides, assist with recruitment, and more.

Other projects have been successful with a smaller leadership team, consisting of just a project manager and lead author. In these cases, the subject expertise of the lead author was well-balanced with the more operational input from the project manager. Together, the duo was able to define the project, create calls, manage content, assess the project's progress, and more.

As you can see, teams come in a different shapes and sizes! And that means that with a bit of reflection on what you have and what you need, you'll be able to find the approach that best suits you.

NEED FURTHER ASSISTANCE?

We hope these suggestions will help you lay the groundwork for your leadership team and set your project up for success from the beginning. We'll continue to add to this guide as we work with more projects, and we welcome your ideas on what else we could add, or your feedback on how these approaches have worked (or not!) for you.

If you have questions, or anything to add, please let us know in the Rebus Community project home.

Recruitment Guide

This section of *The Rebus Guide to Publishing Open Textbooks (So Far)* will help you recruit new team members to join your project, and includes information about creating a call for contributors, where to post these calls, how to onboard a new collaborator, and more. It is licensed under a Creative Commons Attribution 4.0 International License (CC BY) and you are welcome to print this document, make a copy for yourself, or share with others.

If you're looking to build a team around an open textbook project, read through the sections below, and consider the suggestions as you identify areas that need contributors and prepare calls to recruit. Wondering why it's important to recruit people your project? Read our introduction to building a team.

If you have any questions about this, or any other of our guides, please feel free to post them in the Rebus Community project home. This document is an evolving draft, based on our experience managing open textbook projects and community feedback. We welcome your thoughts and contributions, so let us know how it works for you, or if you have any suggestions to improve the guide.

PREPARING TO RECRUIT

Once you've worked through scoping your project, chances are you'll see a number of different places where you could use some extra hands. Before you begin finding people to help, we recommend taking a few important steps to prepare.

DEFINE WHAT YOU NEED

The first step is to think about and write out the details of what you need someone to do, which might take the form of a job description. You might be looking for chapter authors, peer reviewers, or editors, but the job description helps you clearly lay out their specific duties. Try to be **as precise as possible** – you should **list out the various tasks, expectations, and/or responsibilities** of the new contributor. In so doing, you should also get a sense of the time commitment needed on the part of the contributor, include an **estimated time frame** for the job in the description – this is not only for you to keep track of the contributor's workload, but also so that interested volunteers have a sense of how much time they will need to devote to the project.

Once you've been through this process, we suggest you preface the details of the task or job with a brief summary of your project and the work that has been done so far, then finish with information on how to volunteer or participate, and who to contact with any questions. Here's a sample job description for a part editor on an introductory philosophy text.

DECIDE WHO YOU NEED

Once you have a sense of the various tasks that a contributor would need to complete, you can decide on any critical requirements or criteria potential contributors should fulfil. This is a way of ensuring that you find the right person (or people) for the job, and you can be as broad or specific as needed. For instance, if your project is to create an open textbook for introductory philosophy, as in our example above, you might be looking for "faculty or PhD students (ABD)", but you can also list things like "experience teaching first-year philosophy courses" as a requirement for chapter authors.

Depending on the task, however, you might find that these criteria are more of an added bonus than an absolute requirement. For instance, a copyeditor on a Hispanic Literature open textbook project would need to be fluent in Spanish, but a cover designer might not need the same level of fluency.

Once you're clear on any requirements, make sure to add these criteria to the job description so they're clear to anyone interested in volunteering.

FIGURE OUT THE LOGISTICS

Recruiting new collaborators is a team effort (no pun intended), but to avoid any confusion, it's best to **figure out who is responsible for what** to make sure it all goes smoothly. The two major tasks are: sending the calls for contributors and collecting the responses. In some cases, such as during the peer review stage, it might be obvious that the review coordinator is the one in charge, but it might not always be so clear cut. Make sure you speak with your team about who will send out calls for contributors through which channels (everyone should have a hand in here! You all have your own networks to tap into) and who should field the responses and any questions (this should ideally be one or two people at most to avoid crossed wires).

WRITE AND REFINE THE CALL

The most critical piece of the recruitment process is the call inviting collaborators to join the project. The **copy requires a fine balance of information** – too much can disengage (or flat out bore) the user, while too little could leave them hesitant to participate. The key to writing a good call is to be **clear about what you are looking for** – this is where the job description prepared earlier comes in handy!

While there are many details that you could include, be judicious about what people need to know up front. Generally, this will be the information that most directly affects their ability to participate, i.e. **what you want them to do, and when you want them to do it by**. The **deadline for receiving applications** is also an important one. Make sure to include this either at the start or the end of the call, so potential contributors know the latest date to get in touch.

Ideally, the language you use should also **get the reader excited** about the project, and build up a desire for them to take part. You can **play up the community aspect** of the project, and let readers know that in participating, they would join a team of scholars working to build a valuable resource. You could also include a list of other contributors on the project, or the institutions that they are from, to motivate others to join the team. If your project has a **specific mission or unique aspects**, be sure to mention these as well.

Remember to tell the reader *why* they ought to join this project! **What's in it for them?** They might be motivated by the 'good deed' aspect, but readers will also be skimming through the call to see what other benefits they might receive out of working on your project. This could include a byline as an author/editor, other credit in the book, or money. If you have funds available, list any **financial compensation** available for the role.

We also recommend writing a few sentences **encouraging people from traditionally underrepresented groups to apply.** A nod in this direction can help encourage people to apply, and even if you already have a diverse team assembled, more input from people with different experiences can only make the project stronger.

Overall, the **structure of the call** is similar to that of the job description: introduce yourself, and the project briefly, linking to the project summary for more information. Next, mention the specific position you are looking to fill, any requirements for participation, and add a link to the longer job description. Make sure to list the deadline to submit an application and instructions on how to express interest (respond to the email, post in a public forum, join an activity on an online platform, etc.).

Once you and your team are happy with the details and the language, you can start spreading the word!

RECURITING

Now that you know who and what you need, it's time to tell the world! Here's how to get the word out and bring your new recruits on board.

SHARE THE CALL WIDELY, AND CROWDSOURCE EFFORTS

It's important to **get as many eyeballs** on your call as possible! Simple probability says that the more people who see the call, the higher the likelihood of someone responding to it. You and the leadership team should of course share the call yourselves, but also **encourage everyone else on the project** to do the same.

A good place to start when sending out the call is to **crowdsource a list of places** where it could be shared. There are a number of channels where you can share the call, including but not limited to:

- Listservs or mailing lists in your field
- Community listservs or specific mailing lists for traditionally underserved or underrepresented groups
- Your personal and professional networks
- Colleagues and/or OER champions at your institution
- Social media platforms
- Rebus Community newsletter and other mailing lists focused on open education
- Cold calls (not quite a channel, but sometimes worth a shot)

Generally speaking, subject specific mailing-lists and personal networks will help target instructors, faculty, or researchers, and might be best for tasks that require expertise in content like writing, reviewing, beta testing, or adopting. Calls sent on social media or OER in newsletters target a more general group of people, and would be a good channel for activities like formatting, proofreading, or copyediting. Cold calls can be used to target specific people for any activity, but these do require a fair bit of work to find suitable persons to contact, and may not always have the best return on time invested.

RESPONDING TO INTERESTED CONTRIBUTORS

Now that you're getting a flood of responses from interested collaborators (or so we hope!), it's important that you, or the person assigned, **get back to them quickly!** Replying within a day or two is ideal, as it's important not just as a sign of respect to the respondent, but also to capitalise on their interest! Keep in mind that anyone who reaches out is potentially a valuable team member and advocate for the project, even if they don't end up taking on the role you've shared. Also, if people keep asking the same questions, you can take the cue to add more information to the call and/or job description.

If you receive an expression of interest from someone who **doesn't seem right for the position**, be sure to thank them for their interest in your project, and let them know that there may be other roles on the project for which they would be better suited. If they don't meet some of the criteria listed for the position, you can (if needed) lean on this to explain your decision, which is why it's good to have these things in writing in advance.

If you receive an expression of interest from someone who does seem right for the position, but **can't commit to the timeline** or time frame you have set out, again, say thanks first! Let them know that their timelines don't match what you had in mind, but **try to keep them as an option** in case you don't find anyone else. You can suggest continuing the search for the moment, but that you'll reach back if you are unable to recruit someone on your preferred timeline. If you do find an alternate, be sure to update them! And when you do, you should always offer to keep them in the loop for any future tasks and project updates.

Finally, if you don't receive any responses, **don't despair**! Go back to the drawing board and try these:

- See if anything is missing, confusing or unclear in the call or job description
- Ask some colleagues, or existing team members, if they can see anything that might need changing in your copy
- Think about whether the job can be broken into smaller components that are less of a commitment
- Think about timing – if everyone is buried in planning or marking, you might need to wait a while for people to respond

- Revisit your outreach plan, research some other options, and keep sending!

Sometimes it's just a question of keeping at it, making small adjustments, and sending again until you find the right mix.

And now, if you've been keeping track of the combinations, you'll know there's only one left... the magic formula of someone who has responded to your call, is interested in the project, and happy to work within the timeframe outlined. Hooray! Keep reading to see how to onboard this new team member onto your project!

ONBOARDING A NEW RECRUIT

First things first, reply to the contributor **confirming that you would like to welcome them aboard the project**! As with all the other responses, don't forget to thank them for their interest and for volunteering their time. Gratitude and enthusiasm go a long way when you're asking for people's time and energy.

Next, **explain the process and send them all the information** you have about the task they will be completing, and let them know that **questions are welcome**. For instance, if you're recruiting a new author for your project, you should explain the writing and editorial process, share the author guide, point to a model chapter, and confirm deadlines for receiving a first draft. Before they begin working on their task in earnest, you should also share any **MOUs, contracts, or agreements** with the contributor to sign (e.g. our example contributor MOU). Let the new recruit(s) know what **tools or channels of communication** you use, so they know how to contact you or other members on the team. At this point, you could also **share any tracking sheets or other resources** that you are using for managing tasks or the project.

At this stage, it's often a good idea to **set up a call** to go over all of this information, rather than relying solely on email. This is a chance to go through the details and answer any outstanding questions they might have about the project or their role specifically.

In the spirit of collaboration, you should also **introduce the new contributor to the rest of your team**, which can also be done on a call, especially if you're bringing on several people at the same time. Connecting team members with each other, not just the admin. team, is critical to building a community of people around your book and project!

AFTER RECRUITMENT

Now that your team is coming together, it's time to get to work! Your next job is to make sure your new team has everything they need to be successful. Read on for a few tips.

KEEP CONTRIBUTORS INVOLVED

While the hard work of the recruitment portion is over, now is the critical time to ensure that team members are **involved and engaged** as they go about their assigned tasks. While there's always a chance that contributors might drop out of the project for various reasons, you want to make sure that they aren't motivated to do so as a result of how the project is being managed or due to a lack of communication with the larger team.

Clearly communicating with each member on your team is key, so make sure share information that they need to know and are upfront about anything, such as changes in schedule, additional work, delays, etc. Over the course of the project, stay in touch with contributors and **check-in regularly on their tasks**. You should also **send them frequent updates** on the progress being made overall. It's also helpful to **ask for their feedback** on various aspects of the project: their experience could give them added insight or provide a critical perspective that improves how a task is managed or carried out.

For more ideas, take a look at our our **community engagement guide**.

OTHER THINGS TO KEEP IN MIND

While we've laid out a start-to-finish process here, recruitment is **likely to**

be ongoing on your project as you reach and discover various activities where you need more hands on deck. The first time will always be the most work, but from then on, for additional calls, you can reuse a lot of your copy, adjust in response to feedback, reach out through the same channels, leverage your growing team, and your target audience will already know who you are and what you're doing! Besides, it only gets better and easier with practice.

It's also good to know that sometimes you'll end up with **more people** volunteering than anticipated. Take a moment to rethink how many people are needed for the job and whether more people could be beneficial. For example, if you were counting on one author per chapter and you have more interested, they might be interested in collaborating. You can always adjust! No matter what, though, the most important thing is to **keep everyone who reaches out involved** in some way or the other. Even if they're not working on the project directly, anyone interested enough in what you're doing is an asset.

Other times, despite your best efforts, you'll get **fewer people** expressing interest than desired. This is okay – it happens to us all. In these cases, it's a question of quality over quantity, and you can work to make sure you get the most out of those you have. This means making the experience a positive one for them, and being flexible in terms of timelines and workloads to keep things manageable.

Finally, remember that any contributor to the project is a **volunteer** (even if they are financially compensated). They are choosing to give their time and expertise on your project, so do whatever you can to **make it worth their while**, and **recognize their contributions however you can.**

NEED FURTHER ASSISTANCE?

We hope these suggestions will help you prepare, recruit, and onboard new contributors to your project smoothly. We'll continue to add to this guide as we work with more projects, and we welcome your ideas on what else we could add, or your feedback on how these approaches have worked (or not!) for you.

If you have questions, or anything to add, please let us know in the Rebus Community project home.

Roles & Responsibilities

This section of *The Rebus Guide to Publishing Open Textbooks (So Far)* is meant to help you understand all the different players involved in the making of an open textbook or other OER. It is licensed under a Creative Commons Attribution 4.0 International License (CC BY) and you are welcome to print this document, make a copy for yourself, or share with others.

Read through the sections below to get a better sense of the kinds of positions you can have on your team, how responsibilities can be distributed, and think on how best these might apply to your own project. If you have any questions or feedback, please feel free to post them in the Rebus Community project home. This document is an evolving draft, based on our experience managing open textbook projects and community feedback. We welcome your thoughts and contributions, so let us know how it works for you, or if you have any suggestions to improve the guide.

HOW DID WE COME UP WITH THIS LIST?

During our time supporting different kinds of OER projects, we've seen teams take on a number of forms. However, we noticed some patterns emerging in how work has been distributed across these teams. The list below is our attempt at categorising these roles, and should give you an idea of the types of work carried out when publishing an open textbook (or OER), and who is responsible for completing these tasks.

Keep in mind that the roles and responsibilities outlined may not necessarily always be assigned to one person, and that crossover can happen. It's also not likely that every project will have (or need) teams large enough to account for all these roles, so use this list as a guide to decide what is most applicable to your project's needs. Please also note that this list is not comprehensive – it's very likely that this will grow as we hear from you or other teams! So if you see any positions missing from here, please let us know in the Rebus Community project home.

LIST OF ROLES AND ASSOCIATED RESPONSIBILITIES

To start, we'll cross of some of the things that all team members are responsible for. This includes:

- Being nice, compassionate, and a good team player

- Promoting the project widely wherever possible

- Supporting fellow team members in their work

- Meeting their commitments, so that it does not fall upon someone else to complete

These basic standards apply to everyone, and everyone in a team is responsible for committing to them, and holding their fellow teammates accountable.

Beyond this, each of the roles we've detailed below offers up something unique and critical to the creation of the open textbook (or OER). Note that the following list is alphabetical, not in any hierarchical order ('cause you're all important!).

Accessibility Coordinator

All projects should ideally have an accessibility coordinator overseeing whether the resource meets best practices for accessibility. The accessibility coordinator will be responsible for:

- Working with the project manager, lead editor, and lead author to build best practices into working documents, chapter templates and, ultimately, the final content

- Finding and sharing resources on creating accessible content with the team

- Answering (or finding answers to) questions about accessibility from authors and others on the team as they arise

- Recruiting and onboarding an accessibility reviewer (or completing the review themselves)

- Preparing an accessibility statement for the final text, surfacing the work done and any known issues

In some cases, this coordinator can act as an accessibility reviewer as well. Note that this position could be taken by any other member on the team, such as a lead editor or project manager, and they don't necessarily need a lot of expertise themselves – just a willingness to facilitate the accessibility work that needs to be done throughout the creation process.

Accessibility Reviewer

The accessibility reviewer provides critical feedback on whether the resource, either as a whole or at a chapter or section-level, meets accessibility standards. The reviewer's duties include:

- Conducting an accessibility review on final file formats

- Making recommendations for further improvements

- Preparing, or contributing to, an accessibility statement

- Coordinating with the lead author, lead editor, and project manager

Advisor

An advisor is someone not directly involved in the producing the book or resource, but who is involved at a high level and offers advice or input as needed. Their responsibilities might include:

- Providing input on the project's definition and direction, and shaping content at a high level

- Setting broad strategic objectives for the resource
- Making sure that these goals are met
- Ensuring the team includes diverse perspectives, which are also represented in the content created
- Mediating conflict if/as it arises
- Acting as an impartial body and advising the admin team on decisions
- Helping find and recruit volunteers
- Attending meetings or calls with the leadership team
- Promoting the project from conception to publication
- Coordinating with the project manager

Read more about the role of advisors in a leadership team.

Author

The author on an open textbook or OER project is, you've guessed it, responsible for writing or creating the content. They might also have other duties, such as:

- Creating chapter proposals
- Writing chapter outlines
- Attending author calls
- Reading through and following the author guide, chapter template etc.
- Ensuring as best they can that the chapter fits within the larger text
- Writing with best practices around accessibility and inclusive design in mind
- Including relevant media in each chapter and checking permissions
- Creating ancillaries

- Making chapter glossaries, bibliographies, or other materials
- Coordinating with editors and project manager

Beta Tester

A beta tester is either an instructor or a student using a resource in their classroom, typically before the 'official' release of a text, and providing critical feedback, either on the text as a whole or at a chapter or section-level. The beta tester's duties include:

- Conducting a 'trial run' of a text in a classroom setting
- Reading the beta testing guide thoroughly and making sure they understand it
- Providing feedback in line with rubric or other guidelines (contained in a beta testing guide)
- Providing feedback in agreed format and within set timeframes
- Communicating with the beta testing coordinator
- Communicating with authors/editors
- Promoting the book, if they are satisfied with the quality of the resource and see value in it
- (Hopefully!) Adopting the book, if as an instructor they would like to use the book for future courses

Beta Testing Coordinator

Projects can benefit from having a beta testing coordinator overseeing and organizing the beta testing process. The beta testing coordinator will be responsible for:

- Making sure beta testing is completed successfully
- Preparing a beta testing guide and other preparatory documents such as tracking sheets, calls for beta testers, etc.
- Recruiting beta testers

- Providing beta testers with access to documents such as the beta testing guide, tools, and feedback mechanisms
- Acting as a point of contact for anyone involved in the beta testing process
- Managing deadlines, etc. for beta testers
- Liaising between authors or editors and beta testers
- Collecting and collating student and instructor feedback
- Coordinating with the project manager

Champion

This is an unofficial role, but an important one! Champions are the project's biggest cheerleader, both for the internal team and for the external public. They can help with:

- Keeping the team motivated
- Promoting the project
- Providing quotes, snippets, and updates about the project for marketing/promotional materials
- Acting as an audience test-case and asking for clarification on anything that isn't clear
- Helping polish any communications about the project
- Acting as the public face of project, along with the project manager
- Providing input on the project broadly, similar to an advisor
- Helping recruit collaborators to the project and sharing any calls within their network
- Helping find adopters for the final resource
- Being enthusiastic about the project and the team! It goes a long way to making the experience enjoyable for everyone.

Contributor

Contributors on a project will come in many different shapes, and asked to complete many varying tasks. This is a bit of a catch-all term for the kinds of jobs that aren't captured in the other roles, but make not mistake – all contributions are valuable! Broadly, their responsibilities include:

- Performing the task in line with expectations

- Asking questions if the task and expectations are unclear

- Communicating with other contributors, the coordinator, lead editor, lead author, project manager, and the rest of the team.

Coordinator

Similar to the case with contributors, there may be different kinds of task that emerge that don't fit under any of the headings in this list, but someone still needs to be responsible for them. Enter the coordinator! They may be tasked with:

- Clearly defining the task at hand and producing supporting documentation for it

- Recruiting and coordinating with contributors

- Clarifying expectations regarding contributions

- Ensuring any tasks are completed on the agreed timeline

- Coordinating and communicating with the project manager, lead editor, and lead author

Copyeditor

The copyeditor serves a few different purposes on a project, including:

- Reading through the text correcting errors with grammar, punctuation, or sentence structure

- Following and implementing the appropriate style guide for the project

- Reading the text from a layman's perspective and making sure the content is clear, concise, and makes sense (as such, the copyeditor doesn't need to be a subject expert)
- Ensuring that citations are accurate and consistent
- Checking permissions on media or other non-textual elements

Designer

A project may be fortunate enough to have a dedicated designer, and there's no shortage of things they can bring to the table. These include:

- Designing the book cover (and/or resource landing page)
- Creating promotional materials (such as email signatures, infographics, visuals for social media, etc.)
- Creating images, graphics, or videos to be included in the book
- Checking permissions for any media elements used
- Sharing media in final formats and editable files to enable easier remixing
- Designing with accessibility in mind
- Coordinating with the project manager, lead editor, and lead author

Developmental Editor

The developmental editor's main focus on the project is structure – of the concepts and content in each chapter, of the structure of chapters, and of the book overall. While others are focused on what the book should say, the developmental editor is the person making they say it clearly. This includes:

- Providing input on the book's outline, model chapter, chapter templates with an eye to overarching order of content and avoiding duplication of definitions, themes, etc.
- Conducting an intensive start to finish edit of text as a whole

(focusing less on grammar and punctuation and more on cohesion, structure, and working with the content available)

- Looking at existing resources for comparison
- Making sure that each chapter is structured the same as the others
- Ensuring the text fits together cohesively as whole
- Seeing that text serves its purpose (for a particular course, to fill a void in a field, etc.)
- Identifying areas where content is unclear for a subject matter expert to revise

Depending on the nature of the resource, the person in this role, and the time they can commit to the project, the developmental editor might make any necessary adjustments or changes to the text based on the above themselves. However, this work could also be assigned to the lead author(s), lead editor(s), other authors, or another contributor on the project.

Formatter

The formatter's work on an open textbook project will vary greatly depending on your choice of book formatting software (note: we strongly encourage using tools that provide both a web version and offline formats, including editable formats). However, their tasks broadly include:

- Collecting "finished" content (generally finished means reviewed, edited and proofread)
- Formatting content in book formatting software such as Pressbooks
- Standardizing formatting across chapters (headings, text boxes, learning outcomes, images, tables, etc.)
- Conducting a simple pass over content for accessibility, both when formatting content and also in the resource's final file formats

- Exporting the text in various file formats and conducting a visual check

- Entering book metadata

- Coordinating with the lead author, lead editor, and project manager

Instructional Designer

Instructional designers are instrumental towards ensuring that your resource is an effective learning tool. The instructional designer's tasks are varied, including:

- Working with lead editor or lead author on chapter template and preparatory documents (such as the project summary, outline, model chapter, etc.)

- Confirming learning objectives for resource with the project manager, lead author, and lead editor

- Ensure that these learning objectives are served by the content

- Supporting authors, editors, formatters during content creation and responding to questions as they arise

- Making sure text fits needs of target course(s)

Lead Author

The lead author is typically the person writing the bulk of the content for the text, and will work closely with the lead editor. The major duties of the lead author include:

- Preparing a sensible chapter structure, working in tandem with instructional designers or lead editors

- Creating model chapters

- Writing content (generally more than other authors, often most of the book)

- Answering questions from other authors and making judgement calls when necessary

- Creating ancillary materials, or templates others can follow
- Coordinating with the lead editor and project manager

Note that in the absence of a dedicated lead editor, the lead author would likely assume many of the lead editor's responsibilities.

Lead Editor

A lead editor is primarily responsible for setting the vision for the resource, as well as process and workflows related to content creation. The major duties assigned to the lead editor include:

- Crafting the book's outline and structure, and soliciting input on both
- Helping shape processes around content (including creating guides and templates)
- Managing and liaising with any other editors on the team
- Stepping-in when needed, to make decisions about content, or to resolve conflict
- Editing content
- Looking through the text with an expert eye and viewing the resource as a whole throughout the creation process
- Taking charge of promotion and recruitment, and filling in any gaps for authors or section editors
- Being the face of the project, alongside the project manager
- Being a cheerleader to authors and other editors
- Keeping the team focused on broader goals and priorities including diversity, equity, inclusion, accessibility, etc.
- Helping organise and leading team calls
- Running and organizing calls with editors and authors
- Coordinating with the project manager

Project Manager

If you've read any of our other resources, you'll see the words project manager cropping up over and over. As the name suggests, this person is responsible for managing the project – that is, running the process of creating a resource from the beginning, all the way to release (in the traditional publishing world, the managing editor would be a good equivalent for this role). It's a big job, but can be shared, and is critical to a project's success. Duties include:

- Keeping track of everything on the project to ensure that the resource is on its way to completion

- Keeping everyone on track with their tasks, including sharing supporting documents, answering questions and sending reminders

- Managing project-related documents and tools

- Managing the public listing on the Rebus Community platform

- Coordinating team calls

- Coordinating recruitment and calls for contributors

- Managing team communication and keeping the whole team up-to-date as things progress

- Creating and managing timelines and schedules

- Identifying gaps or problems in the process, and ensuring these get resolved

- Being the first point of contact for the project

- Creating a welcoming, supportive environment for all members of the team

Ultimately, the project manager is what we like to refer to as the all-seeing eye on the project, who knows what is happening, when it's happening and who's doing it. This kind of coordination is so important to keep the project on track and make sure that everyone has what they need to be contributing.

The project manager is also very much like a chameleon in that they adapt based on the project's needs. They can step in to work on any smaller teams within the project, help pick up the slack, amplify calls, coordinate schedules, etc. to keep the project moving. Given the flexible nature of a project manager's work, it's good to note that this can easily be a full-time undertaking (so be cautious about doubling up this role with other big jobs like lead author!) although that may not always be the case.

Proofreader

The proofreader conducts a final read-through of the text to:

- Find and fix typos, small errors, etc.
- Check spelling, grammar, and punctuation

Researcher

A project may have a general researcher at hand or a dedicated one for copyright and permissions (for images, media, extensively quoted texts, remixed texts, etc.). Regardless of the type of researcher you have on your team, their responsibilities broadly include:

- Getting clear instructions on what the project needs and locating them (this could be images, videos, public domain texts, examples etc.)
- Checking permissions and copyright, and obtaining permissions where necessary (note: we discourage relying too heavily on one-off permissions, so as to avoid complications for downstream users adapting your text)
- Creating a clear and accurate list of permissions, licenses, and attributions in the final text
- Coordinating with the project manager

Review Coordinator

Some projects will benefit from having a review coordinator overseeing and organizing the peer review process. The review coordinator will be responsible for:

- Preparing a review guide and other preparatory documents such as tracking sheets, calls for reviewers, etc.
- Recruiting reviewers
- Providing reviewers with access to documents such as review guide and tools
- Acting as a point of contact for anyone involved in the review process
- Managing deadlines, etc. for reviewers
- Making sure peer review is successfully completed
- Liaising between authors or editors and reviewers
- Writing the review statement
- Coordinating with the project manager

Reviewer

The peer reviewer is a subject expert who provides critical feedback on the resource, either as a whole or at a chapter or section-level. The reviewer's duties include:

- Reading review guide thoroughly and making sure they understand it
- Providing feedback in line with review rubric & project specific questions (contained in the review guide)
- Providing feedback in agreed format and within set timeframes
- Communicating with the review coordinator
- Communicating with authors/editors (if not part of an anonymous review)

- Promoting the book, if they are satisfied with the quality of the resource and see value in it

- Adopting the book, if they would like to do so

Section Editor or Subject Editor

This editor is a subject matter expert for one section of the book, or for a number of chapter that fall under their expertise. Their responsibilities include:

- Crafting outlines and deciding what content is covered, along with the lead editor

- Helping create guides and templates

- Recruiting authors and reviewing applications

- Liaising with authors, conducting check-ins, and sending reminders with them

- Editing content within their section

- Provide input on other sections in the text

- Helping recruit authors for other sections

- Coordinating with other editors and the project manager

- Coordinating review on their section (optional)

NEED FURTHER ASSISTANCE?

We hope these suggestions help to clarify the roles and responsibilities of those in making an open textbook or OER, and what their particular contributions include. We'll continue to add to this guide as we work with more projects, and we welcome your ideas on what else we could add, or your feedback on how these approaches have worked (or not!) for you.

If you have questions, or anything to add, please let us know in the Rebus Community project home.

 *This work is licensed under the Creative Commons Attribution 4.0 International License.*

Managing Volunteers

This section of *The Rebus Guide to Publishing Open Textbooks (So Far)* will help you as a project manager to ensure that the volunteers and collaborators on your project are motivated and keen to stay involved, and that they are fairly recognised and rewarded for their work, even if it is on a volunteer basis. It is licensed under a Creative Commons Attribution 4.0 International License (CC BY) and you are welcome to print this document, make a copy for yourself, or share with others.

If you're looking for tips on how best to manage a group of volunteers, consider the suggestions below as you're forming and managing your team. If you have any questions about this, or any other of our guides, please feel free to post them in the Rebus Community project home. This document is an evolving draft, based on our experience managing open textbook projects and community feedback. We welcome your thoughts and contributions, so let us know how it works for you, or if you have any suggestions to improve the guide.

FIRST OF ALL, WHO OR WHAT IS A PROJECT MANAGER?

As the name suggests, this person is responsible for managing the project – that is, the process of seeing the resource all the way to release (in the traditional publishing world, the managing editor would be a good equivalent). The project manager's duties are wide ranging (read more about them in our Roles & Responsibilities guide), but for the purposes of this discussion, we'll focus on their role managing a team of volunteers. This involves:

- Interacting with volunteers & being their point of contact on a project
- Managing their task assignments, deadlines, workloads, etc.
- Providing supporting documentation and guidance on expectations
- Establishing project norms for recognising work
- Mediating and resolving tensions or conflict

Project managers are of course not alone in handling these, and other in the leadership team have a big part to play, too. Overall, those running a project are responsible for making sure everyone involved (including themselves) is supported throughout the process and recognised for their time and commitment.

WHO ARE VOLUNTEERS, AND WHY ARE THEY IMPORTANT?

There are numerous benefits to having a team around your project – to help share the workload, keep you motivated, and improve the quality and impact of the final resource. Without a team, you may not be able to complete your project, or might take a very long time to do so. Take a look at our overview of building a team for more on why teams are important.

Given the need for extra hands, most teams will likely have at least some volunteers involved. Volunteers are, to put it simply, people who believe in your project and are willing to devote their time and expertise to it without much (or any) financial compensation. The fact that many volunteers will be expending time, energy, and more on your project without any payment, makes their contributions all the more valuable.

It's also important to remember that even those who are compensated in some way, or who have a mandate in their day job to support OER (so might not be officially considered volunteers) are likely to be putting in more than they are paid to do. Many of the people involved are likely to be contributing to a project because they believe in it, and it's important for managers to be aware of that and not take advantage. Project managers, and indeed the whole team, should recognise the value of the labour put into a project and find ways to make sure it is recognised and rewarded in a variety of ways, not just financial compensation.

Volunteers, whether officially designated as such or not, come with all sorts of wonderful skills that you might not have yourself – so recognize the value they bring, and most importantly, don't take them for granted!

"MANAGING" VOLUNTEERS SOUNDS TRICKY…

The truth is, managing volunteers who are providing free labour is tricky, and ethically complex. While volunteers do tend to participate in projects out of belief in the mission, managers have to balance leveraging that passion with not exploiting it. The labour that goes into creating open textbooks is immensely valuable, but often isn't compensated in the lingua franca of most work arrangements: money. As a result, managers should be thinking of other ways to compensate and recognise the work done, but it can be an uncomfortable experience if you're new to it.

These different motivators and exchanges can also make it difficult for managers to feel like they have the authority to ask a lot of volunteers. It's also not a totally unfounded concern – it can sometimes be tough to keep people on track, especially when you have neither stick nor carrot to spur them on. There's no ready answer to this conundrum, but it's something to be aware of and to figure out in your context.

In addition, hierarchies and power relations within teams can be non-traditional. You may find yourself as a project manager or lead, tasked with overseeing a group of volunteers who are your seniors elsewhere in your work. You may find these volunteers asserting their position within the team, leading to a situation where there are 'too many cooks in the kitchen.' Especially in these cases, it's important that you remember that this is still your project, and that you need to be able to lay down the law as needed, albeit diplomatically.

Managing volunteers can also prove difficult as people generally have other things going on in their work and personal lives, sometimes making it hard to keep track of them (and to keep them on track!). In some situations, you may stop hearing from a volunteer entirely, which may be a sign that they are no longer participating in the project, but they might also pop up again later and still be keen to contribute. In other cases, you might find that the volunteers' work or their behaviour itself is not up to scratch, which needs to be handled carefully.

Perhaps the trickiest part about managing volunteers is the emotional labour involved. As part of this work, you will need to form professional relationships with your teammates; take into account volunteers' personalities when interacting with them; be conscious of individuals' egos and emotions; rephrase and rearticulate seemingly straightforward communications into something more tactful; patiently send out reminders; repeat and relay information many times over; and more. As a manager, you need to see to the overall well-being of your group, but also not at the expense of yourself. This is a hard balance to achieve, but hopefully the tips and suggestions below will help!

...BUT YOU CAN STILL BE A GOOD MANAGER

The best way to be a good manager to your volunteers is to be open and transparent about the project and related tasks. Make sure to give your volunteers all the information they need upfront, and be clear about what you expect them to deliver. Setting clear expectations at the start of the project, and keeping the lines of communication open throughout the process is key.

Here are some other strategies you might find useful:

- Ask all your volunteers to **sign a Memorandum of Understanding (MOU)** at the outset of their involvement in the project, to clarify their roles and responsibilities in relation to the larger team. You can use our MOU template and adapt it to your project, or create your own. In the spirit of collaboration, make sure to sign the MOU yourself, so volunteers are aware that the same expectations and standards apply equally to them and you – and make sure you follow through.

- If volunteers have any questions for you, either at the start of the project or later down the line, be patient with them and do your best to **answer their queries, even if the information is available to them elsewhere**. As mentioned, volunteers will likely be juggling many different tasks, projects, and responsibilities, so they might forget details related to your project or get confused with their specific task. Here too, be patient and kind with interacting with them – it will make their experience of working on the project all the better! And on a practical note, keep as many of these exchanges public as possible, so everyone benefits from the responses, make sure any questions really are answered in your documentation (updating them if need be), and maintain a running list of FAQs that you can point people to.

- If you have any questions, concerns, or hesitations about a particular volunteer, try to **vet them up front** by asking for a CV, writing sample, or relevant materials. Also, try to **reflect and think critically about why you're hesitating** – just because they might not be who you expected to show up doesn't mean they won't be an asset. Different backgrounds, experiences and expertise can all contribute to a stronger project.

- Throughout the course of the project, be sure to **recognise your volunteers and their time with consistent gratitude**. Acknowledgment of their contributions and commitment goes a long way.

- Make the experience an enjoyable one! Do your best to **include some informal social time** to catch up, discuss the weather and say hellos when you meet, during calls, or digitally, before getting down to business.

- **Give regular updates to all volunteers** about the work taking place elsewhere on the project – this helps to make them feel connected to the bigger picture and can help motivate them to complete their own contribution. Regardless of a volunteer's contribution to the project, this helps to make them feel like they are part of the team working towards a common goal.

- Keep in mind that people on your team may be from different backgrounds, and as such, might face different challenges or have different needs when completing a task. It's important that you don't force your way or method of working on your fellow volunteers, and instead **let them decide how best they want to forge ahead with a task.** Remember that just because something is different, doesn't mean that it is wrong.

- **If someone's contribution isn't up to scratch, be tactful, constructive, and look for other ways they can participate**. You don't have an obligation to include something in your project that you and your leadership team does not want to, but if you're uncomfortable conveying this to a volunteer, ask others to help you.

- All along the way, it's good to **show volunteers that you appreciate their work by rewarding them however possible**. This doesn't necessarily need to be in the form of money (although paying people if you can is always a good thing!), but can be simple things like:

  - giving volunteers good (impressive-sounding) titles
  - including names, biographies, and relevant links in promotional materials and the final work
  - writing recommendation letters
  - sending them print copies of the text or other tokens once it's released
  - and of course, if you are in a position to compensate them financially for their contribution, they are sure to appreciate it.

Most importantly, try to be understanding and empathetic about your volunteers. As a manager, you should provide volunteers with a clear platform to voice their concerns, and also be clear about what decision-making processes look like in the team. Let volunteers know what your responsibility is to them and the project. Tell them how much time you plan to devote to the project, so they can see you meeting their commitments with your own. Being a good manager is ultimately about being a good team player and coach – you set your team up to succeed, and be there to help if needed.

WHAT IF SOMETHING GOES WRONG?

Even if you follow all the suggestions outlined above, it's unlikely that your project will run smoothly and perfectly from start to finish (if it does, tell us how in the Rebus Community project home!). So if something goes wrong, no matter how big or small, don't stress. These things happen, and your first reaction as a manager should be to: take a deep breath, and sleep on the issue. Try not to respond immediately either in anger, worry, or panic, but try to take a bit of time to think it over. Being a manager also means being responsive and adapting the plan as you go, and there's always a solution somewhere.

Here are some other strategies you might look to:

- Depending on the nature of the issue, it might help to go **back to your preparatory documents**, such as the project summary, outline, MOU, etc. Consider these documents as evidence of your project work, and sift through them for clarity and reassurance. They also provide confirmation if there is disagreement on something that was set out early on.

- If a problem emerges with a volunteer, try to set up some time to meet them and **talk through the issue face-to-face**, instead of over text or email. Turn to your admin and advisory teams for help, but try not to make the volunteer feel like you are ganging up against them. Your first goal should be to attain clarity over the situation, and not to make a decision or pass judgment.

- If an issue related to content crops up, for instance if an author wants to back out of the project during the editing/review phase, or if an author doesn't want to make important changes requested by a reviewer or editor, look back to your MOU and confirm the license on content submitted. More often than not, if the content was licensed CC BY, it can be salvaged in some way to be useful for the project if you decide that's best. However, depending on the situation, it might not be good form to include contested content even if you have the legal right to do so. Use your judgement, and defer to the content creator.

- If a volunteer is acting a crass or rude manner to you or anyone else on the project, it's within your rights to **ask them to leave the project**. As a manager, you are responsible for the team overall, and should stand-up against anyone disobeying the team's ground rules. You can do so politely, but stand your ground and protect your fellow collaborators. Again, look for backup from your leadership team if you need it.

- It's good to acknowledge that in some situations, you might be the person who messed up. In this case, be up front about where things went wrong, and **take responsibility for your actions**. Then, do what you can to look for solutions and to fix the error. Don't be afraid to ask for help, from your team and from the community at large!

Lastly, look to the community not only for help in situations, but also for advice and counsel. Talk to other project managers, find out their experiences, learn from their successes and failures, and share your own stories. Remember that even if you're the only manager on your project, you're not alone in the community!

DON'T FORGET TO LOOK AFTER YOURSELF

Managing a group of people is hard work, and you might get used to putting yourself in the backseat and keeping the project or volunteers at the forefront. While the project and other volunteers are important, you are too! We wanted to end this section with a short reminder to make sure you're managing your own time and well-being carefully too.

Be nice to yourself along the way, and remember that you are also volunteering your energy on the project. Even if you're being paid to act as a project manager, your time and effort are still valuable. Take breaks from the project every now and then and try to build in time to spend on other things – managing a project can be a lot of work, but it should also be a positive experience for you, both personally and professionally.

NEED FURTHER ASSISTANCE?

We hope these suggestions will help you be an effective project manager. We'll continue to add to this guide as we work with more projects, and we welcome your ideas on what else we could add, or your feedback on how these approaches have worked (or not!) for you.

If you have questions, or anything to add, please let us know in the Rebus Community project home.

Contributor MOU Template

MEMORANDUM OF UNDERSTANDING [PROJECT TITLE]

[*Project Name*] is a collaborative project, aimed at creating a quality open textbook/open resource for [*audience*]. [*Optional: add a few more sentences about the project and its mission*].

This memorandum of understanding (MOU) lays out the contributor expectations, licensing information, and other conditions of participation. All members of the team are asked to read through and agree to the terms. Any questions or concerns can be addressed to the project manager: [*Project Manager name + contact details*].

1. Role expectations

In this section, write out any expectations for specific kinds of contributors, e.g. authors, reviewers, lead editors, etc.

2. Licensing

All content (writing, images, charts, videos, etc.) created for inclusion in this textbook, as well as ancillary materials (slide decks, assignments, in-class exercises etc. **with the exception of question banks**), are to be licensed under a Creative Commons Attribution 4.0 International License (CC BY 4.0). In accordance, all authors and other creators retain the copyright to their contributions, and by signing below, grant a CC-BY 4.0 license to all content created for this project.

3. Edits, updates, and revisions

All team members understand and accept that the content they produce in the context of this project may be edited, updated, reviewed, and otherwise altered over the course of the publishing process. Authors/creators will have the opportunity to address significant recommended changes or additions following peer review and/or developmental editing, and retain the right to remove their name from the published version at any time.

4. Team participation

All participants are expected to be engaged, respectful team members. This includes:

- Participating in project discussions, decision making processes, team calls/webinars, and other activities as requested

- Ensuring you meet agreed all upon deadlines, or offer as much notice as possible if you require an extension. If, for any reason, you need to pull out of the project, this should also be indicated to the admin team promptly

- Participating in promotional activities and actively leveraging your own network wherever possible to attract contributors and adopters

- Treating all members of the team with respect, in words and actions

- Engaging with and furthering the project goals

5. Recognition for contributors

This section should state what recognition is offered to contributors, e.g.: "All contributors will be named in the acknowledgements section of the final publication unless they request to be removed. This attribution will include their name and institutional affiliation, and link to a profile or other professional site of their choosing."

6. Termination

The project admin team reserves the right to terminate participation in the project at any time if a contributor is:

- Not fulfilling their agreed upon obligations in a timely manner
- Failing to treat other members of the team with respect
- Otherwise disrupting or negatively impacting the success of the project and team

If a team member is asked to leave the project, any submitted work may be retained and completed/expanded by another contributor in accordance with the conditions of the CC-BY 4.0 license. In this instance, the original creator will still be credited in the final text unless they request to have their name removed.

7. Contributor agreement

I, ______________, agree to the terms of participation stated above.

Signed: _________________________________ Date: ________________

Engagement Guide

This guide is meant to help you with contributor engagement, so that the team around your open textbook project remains active and committed to seeing the book all the way through to publication. It is licensed under a Creative Commons Attribution license (CC BY) and you are welcome to print this document, make a copy for yourself, or share with others.

Please read through sections below, and consider the suggestions as you are planning your project's timeline and estimating workloads, or to help move along a project that is lagging or stalled. If you have any questions, please feel free to reach out to us on the Rebus Community project home. This document is based on our experience managing open textbook projects, and we welcome your feedback and additional suggestions.

WHY DOES ENGAGEMENT MATTER?

In the open textbook projects that Rebus has supported, engagement has been a key factor determining the project's advancement or success. Most projects saw some initial interest, buzz, and activity during the first few weeks. However, we noticed that this can die down fairly quickly, and in some cases, where a project has stretched out for too long, we've lost a few contributors along the way. It falls on the project leads to make a conscious effort to keep participants engaged.

Our most successful projects have had an active community of participants – authors, editors, proofreaders, copy editors, reviewers, formatters, leads, other volunteers – who conversed with each other often with updates about their tasks or the project more generally.

These projects found a way to ensure participants knew the work they were doing was valuable and part of a larger effort. They also enabled contributors to connect with a larger community of practice in their subject. We found that public-facing projects with a lot of activity acted as social proof for current and potential collaborators: encouraging new people to get involved with the project, and fuelling those already on board to complete the tasks that they had signed up to do.

Ultimately, while engagement helped drive projects forward, for some participants, it was the connections they made with others, and the conversations/discussions they had that they valued. Contact between authors, between editors and authors, between authors and formatters, and similar, created a sense of community, even mentorship, among participants. The project leads for the *Media Innovation and Entrepreneurship* open textbook formed a community of practice and held biweekly calls with those adopting or teaching with the book.

> "Many thanks...for the gift to join you in such a fascinating intellectual and collaborative journey for making the Open Textbook on *Media Innovation & Entrepreneurship* a dynamic learning, writing, and mentoring experiment. Along with the open textbook and the upcoming instructors' manual, I think you are also helping to create a very dynamic network and community of practice."
>
> **—Betty Tsakarestou, author and assistant professor at Panteion University**

SUGGESTIONS FOR ENGAGEMENT

Below are some ways in which you can try to create an engaged community around your project. This list will continue to grow as we learn from other projects and we welcome suggestions if you've had success managing similar volunteer projects.

Introduce your team to one another

This sounds very straightforward, but make sure to introduce members of the team to one another. It's not uncommon to be juggling several lines of communication between yourself as the team lead and many participants, but creating connections across the project is just as important for keeping people engaged. If you're located in the same city, you could try to arrange an in-person meet. However, most projects tend to involve participants from all around the world – so a simple email or video call to introduce the team to one another will suffice!

If you're not the project lead, but an editor of a particular part or section of the book, you could send a similar email to the authors in your part. The email should welcome individuals to the team, and could even include links to shared resources such as the project's timeline.

Acknowledge different working and communication styles, and involve your team in project planning

If you're the project lead, it's especially important to keep in mind that members of your team may not have the same working or communication style. These kinds of things vary across people and cultures, and if you have a global team, you can't expect everyone to switch to your default. Instead, you should discuss preferences and expectations at the start of the project, and invite members to help plan the project timeline and tasks with you. This may help to avoid conflict or disengagement down the line, and help you better gauge when an issue might be arising.

You should also discuss communication preferences with team members early on – is email okay, or are calls better? What kind of response time is expected? Respect these preferences, and as project lead, ask your team to do the same. Sharing this information up front, to whatever extent possible, will help your team understand one another, leading towards smoother interactions and fewer frustrations.

Share examples – model chapters/outlines/abstracts

Make sure everyone has model chapters/outlines/abstracts or whatever else they're being asked to submit. This can ease the cognitive load of getting started, and help ensure consistency in what's submitted. Where possible, it's also good to select this model content from what has already been submitted or created by a project lead and share it with the others –

this also adds the little nudge that others are further ahead, which can help get people moving!

Encourage contributors to post questions/share drafts

Wherever possible, we ask contributors to share their drafts or ask any questions that they have on a public-facing channel, such as the Rebus Community forum or in Google docs shared with other authors. This helps other members of the team keep track of various tasks, reduces the work of having to answer the same questions many times over, gives people examples to work from, and acts as a subtle reminder to those who may be behind on their deadlines.

Send individual emails/ conduct one-on-one calls

If general reminder emails aren't getting much of a response, try individual emails or one-on-one calls with the team leads. If a particular contributor has dropped off the radar, or you're not sure they're seeing the emails you're sending to the whole team, check in with them personally to see how they're getting on. A short note can do the trick, and it may just be that they're having a busy couple of weeks, but the response rate is generally higher with this approach!

Put together an FAQ, and let others add to it

If you find the same questions or concerns are coming up from multiple people, consider putting together an FAQ to share with other contributors. You can give contributors editing privileges, and encourage them to add to the list, so the burden of updating the list doesn't fall solely on you. Also consider whether any of these questions could be addressed in your author/editor/contributor guide or project summary and add to them as needed.

Hold regular calls with your team

You may also want to hold a call with your contributors, or an office hours-style drop in session. Encouraging attendance at these can also help develop the community feeling, which helps keep people invested and responsible to each other to fulfill their commitments. These calls may be structured around each chapter, connecting authors and instructors giving feedback for example, or each phase of the project ("Two weeks until submission deadline! Help!") or be an open space for feedback and questions as needed.

Dissuade the drop-outs: instead, encourage participation in less time-consuming tasks...

If at any point it looks like someone might be backing out, suggest that they could instead take on a different role, perhaps acting as a reviewer instead of an author, or help to promote the book down the line. And always ask if they want to stay up to date as things progress! You can contact them again when you're looking for other kinds of contributions or releasing the book. Sharing updates or notifications when the book is available is a good way to acknowledge their interest in the project, even if they haven't been able to commit to it entirely.

... but remember that not everyone will stay involved, and that's okay!

Contributors always have the option to say no and withdraw if they're not able to participate in a project. If they're interested enough to have signed up in the first place, it's worth trying to keep them in the loop, but they might not always want that. It can be disappointing, but if someone does have to bow out completely, remember that we all have competing priorities, and you never know what may be happening on their end. Be respectful of that, and wish them well. There will be plenty more people out there with the time to give to your project to whom you can shift your focus.

NEED FURTHER ASSISTANCE?

We hope these suggestions will help you form a robust, committed community around your project. We'll continue to add to this guide as we work with more projects, and we'd welcome your ideas on what else we could add, or your feedback on how these approaches have worked (or not!) for you.

If you have questions or anything to add, please let us know in the Rebus Community project home.

PROJECT SCOPING

Project Scoping Summary

If you have decided to create an open textbook project, you might be wondering where to begin. Getting started, whether it's your first or fiftieth time, is always the hardest part! But you can begin by gathering your team around you, then start sketching out the high level details of the project, setting goals, drafting timelines, and more. This is an exciting part of the process, where you get to really think about what your project will look like, and a lot of the work you put in up front will serve you well over the coming months.

> **Underlying principles**
>
> **Creating an open textbook is about more than just writing the content.** There's a lot that goes into making a book, from planning, editing, review, formatting, marketing, and more. Part of scoping is to think about the whole publishing process, so you know what's coming. It might seem like more work than you anticipated, but this is why a good team is important, and there are lots of resources out there to support you.
>
> **Target audiences should include all readers, so keep accessibility front of mind from the start.** Good accessibility practices benefit all readers, and the more that can be done during the creation process, the less remediation will be needed later. Commit to good accessibility practices from day one in concrete ways by stating it as a project goal, building it into guides, educating yourself and connecting with experts.
>
> **Reflect on the motivations and values that drive you as a person, and**

see how you can build them into the textbook. Highlighting them as unique aspects of your project and emphasizing their importance will also help your collaborators feel like they are working towards a larger goal. The reasons why this project is important enough for you to commit to it will almost always resonate strongly with others — so share your story.

Remember that you're not in this alone. Making books is not a solo effort by the author, so make sure to find your community and let them support you. They are there to believe in your project's purpose, set it up for success, celebrate milestones, and help pick you up when you think you're not making as much progress as you'd like.

Plan, revise, and plan again. Take the time to make a plan up front. Prepare timelines, draft book outlines, map key concepts, strategize marketing plans so you can check-in regularly to see if you're meeting targets, and if not, recalibrate! Clear project documentation also means that newcomers can get on board quickly, and you can always refer back to what you've written to keep on track.

Who's Involved?

While your team will continue to grow as your project progresses, it's the leadership team that will be most involved during this phase. The leadership can consist of an admin team to help with more day-to-day tasks, and an advisory team to guide the process at a higher-level, but can also be less formal – the important thing is that there are a core set of people committed to establishing the project. Learn how to build a leadership team in this section of our guide.

An admin team may include:

- Librarians interested in or in charge of developing OER at your institution

- Instructional designers or others from your institution's centre for teaching and learning

- Colleagues or graduate students in your department

- Collaborators on other projects from outside your institution

- Authors or editors already attached to the project

An advisory team may include some of the above, as well as:

- Senior experts or mentors in your field

- Anyone you know with experience publishing textbooks or open textbooks

- Community advisors (this is crucial is you are working on content relating to/impacting a specific community, especially marginalized communities)

- Subject librarians

- Instructors with experience teaching the course for which the resource is intended

Key Tactics

If you're working on an open textbook project, here are some things to do at the very start in order to be better prepared to manage and execute the publishing process:

- Read about the publishing process, and what really goes into making books (this Guide is a great place to start!).

- Work to articulate why your project is important to you, and share this with your team, along with clear expectations about their roles in the project. Keep this documented and read it over and share it whenever you need a reminder.

- Keep a public project listing with key information like book summary, audience, reading level, licenses, target release date, etc. The public

> listing will be the first place you point people to in communications to learn about the project, so make it clear and keep it up to date!
>
> - Start creating the book's outline, including any necessary context or framing up front, plus a list of chapters with descriptions, pedagogical outcomes, and the types of features or elements that will recur through the text.
>
> - Work with your team to create a rough timeline – this can and likely will change over time, but plotting a first version will help you estimate timing and give you some initial milestones to work to.
>
> - Ask for help when you need it. Look to your institution, colleagues, students, the Rebus Community and the academic community more broadly to help.
>
> - Distribute the workload among your team members and look for other possible assistance. There may be specific resources, grants, or funding opportunities available to you, so keep an eye out.
>
> - Decide on the various tools you will be using for project management, communication, writing, editing, review, and formatting.

Thinking about the process of creating the book from the very start, and planning things out early will only make it easier for you and your team down the line. While it may seem overwhelming at first, work through it together, and your future selves will thank you for it!

Read on to explore the whys and hows of scoping out and starting on your open textbook project.

Project Scoping Overview

Congratulations on the start of your new project!

This section of *The Rebus Guide to Publishing Open Textbooks (So Far)* is meant to help you with the initial steps of your project, such as setting up your leadership team, defining the project, creating an outline, and more. It is licensed under a Creative Commons Attribution 4.0 International License (CC BY) and you are welcome to print this document, make a copy for yourself, or share with others.

Please read through the sections below, and consider the suggestions as you begin planning your project's timeline and estimating workloads. If you have any questions, please feel free to post them in the Rebus Community project home. This document is an evolving draft, based on our experience managing open textbook projects and community feedback. We welcome your thoughts and contributions, so let us know how it works for you, or if you have any suggestions to improve the guide.

CONSIDERATIONS WHEN GETTING STARTED

Where to begin?! Getting started with your open textbook project, whether it's your first or fiftieth, is always the hardest part. Before you get into full-swing with your project, here are some things to think about.

First up, you should know about some of the (many) things that go into publishing a textbook: planning, project management, recruiting, writing, editing, peer review, formatting, accessibility review, printing, and marketing. Some of these might happen simultaneously, and not every project will take the same approach to all of them, but remember, **there is more to creating an open textbook than just writing the content**.

It's also important that you **keep accessibility top of mind** from the very beginning of your project. Thinking about accessibility as you are planning, writing, editing, revising, and formatting content will ensure that everyone can access your book from the moment of publication. Good accessibility practices benefit *all* readers, and the more that can be done during the creation process, the less remediation will be needed later.

You can also reflect at the beginning of your project what other **motivations and values** you bring to the table, and how you can build them into your open textbook. This might mean building a diverse and/ or international team, developing content that reflects the experiences of your students, or pushes the boundaries of traditional teaching practices.

With all that in mind, let's acknowledge it right away: you'll likely find yourself saying at many stages of the process *"this is a lot of work"*. Creating an open textbook is no minor feat, but we want you to remember that **you don't have to do it alone**. There are plenty of people who are willing to assist you, so **you shouldn't be afraid to ask for help**. Look to your institution, colleagues, students, the Rebus Community and the academic community more broadly to help. There may also be specific resources, grants, or funding opportunities available to you, so keep an eye out! You should also be sure to step away from the project and take time off as needed – it's important to look after yourself and keep things in perspective. Remember that it's okay to put other priorities before your work on the project and deadlines.

Finally, your project, and the work that goes into making your open textbook, is worth talking about! We strongly believe that **marketing is built into every stage of the publishing process**, and starts right now. You may want to make announcements that you're beginning a new project, that you're excited about what will happen, and that you'll keep others updated along the way. This is not only a great way to gather contributors and encourage eventual adoptions of the textbook, but also a good way to celebrate small victories and milestones along the way. Onward!

LEADERSHIP TEAM

Forming a leadership team around your project is just as important as curating the content for your book. With the right leadership team, you can distribute responsibilities, keep the project driving forward, and ensure that it runs smoothly. There are many different approaches to forming this team, and not everyone has to sign up for a big workload. You may want to have a core leadership team that focuses on the project's day-to-day activities, as well as an advisory team to help steer the project in the right direction as needed.

Once you have recruited all the members for your leadership team, we recommend that you begin with introductions and **assigning clear roles**. For instance, you may be the team's Project Manager, and may want to assign roles such as Lead Editor, Lead Author to other members. Each role comes with its own set of **responsibilities**, so make sure to lay these out when assigning roles. As Project Manager, you may be responsible of keeping track of the project and ensuring that it is on track for publication. Other responsibilities might include communicating project updates to the team, scheduling and running meetings, and assisting with recruitment efforts.

Laying out the responsibilities upfront will avoid members from taking on more than they can commit to, and help you clearly **distribute the project workload**. Creating an open textbook is no small feat. It takes a lot of time, and can often be more work than initially anticipated, but with a competent, committed project team, where tasks are evenly distributed, you won't have to worry about too much falling on your plate or feeling overloaded.

As you move forward with your project, keep in mind **other resources** that you could tap for assistance. You could look for students, colleagues, research or teaching assistants, and other volunteers to help with certain tasks. The Rebus Community is also a great way to find people outside your own network to help with different pieces of your project.

And finally, it's important that you **find your community and support**

team. Having a community of people who believe in your project's purpose, want it to succeed as much as you do, can celebrate milestones, and can pick you up when you think you're not making as much progress is key. Start with your leadership team, and build the community as you get your project off the ground. You won't regret it!

PROJECT DEFINITION

Once you have your leadership and advisory teams together, you can start getting into the details of what your project is all about. **Defining your project** is important not only because it helps you and your team understand what you're working towards, but also as it helps provide vital information and framing about the project to those interested in participating. By being as clear and detailed as possible upfront, you can be sure that collaborators coming on to your project at any time have the same understanding, and know exactly where they can contribute.

There's no limit to the amount of information you could include on your project's public listing page, but we recommend starting off with a few sentences **explaining why this project is important**. Your project might be the first of its kind in a particular field, model a new approach to a certain course, or it might just be exactly what you need for your own teaching. Highlighting any unique aspects of your project and emphasising its importance will help your collaborators feel like they are working towards a larger goal.

You should also include a brief **summary of your project**, and of the open textbook that you are working to create. This needn't be very long – a few paragraphs should suffice!

At this stage, you'll also need to make some **high-level decisions** about your project. For instance, you'll need to decide what **license** to apply to your book, what **audience** you would like the book to target, and at what **reading level** content should be aimed. In cases where projects are receiving grants or funding from organizations, you may need to adhere to the requirements in the contract. As you finalize this information, make sure it's clearly recorded and shared with everyone on the team.

One of the final tasks is to **prepare a rough timeline** that outlines the various stages of the process. It's crucial for you and your team to have an idea of how long tasks take, and when their contributions might be due. We've realized from our work on numerous projects that timelines are never set in stone, and that no matter how hard you try, things can often take longer than planned. So try to revisit, refine, and revise the timeline periodically, and update your team of any changes.

OUTLINE

The next step after writing out your project description is to create an outline for your book. Just as the project definition provides the **necessary information and framing** about your project, the outline will do the same for the textbook. We encourage you to prepare an outline at this stage, and before you begin recruiting authors or other contributors, because you have a clearer sense of the project's goals and the type of resource you are hoping to create.

The outline itself can be fairly simple. It should, of course, contain a **list of all the chapters** to be included in the book, along with **detailed descriptions** of each. Writing out descriptions of the chapters will help you map out the content in your book, and ensure the scope for each is clearly defined and within the scope of your project. You may choose to have individual authors develop the outlines for their chapters, but whenever this happens, making sure they are consistent will help ensure that the final text is cohesive.

It's also helpful to include **features or elements that will recur through the text**, such as case studies, learning objectives, assignments, etc. If possible, you can briefly sketch the structure of a model chapter which includes all these elements. You can also use the outline as an opportunity to **map key concepts** that will be covered in the book, so that they are not repeated in different chapters.

Lastly, you can consider the **pedagogical outcomes** of the book, and think of ways to gesture towards these in each chapter. Doing so may prompt you to rework chapter descriptions or add standard elements, but these changes will be crucial to ensuring that the resource becomes a valuable one for students.

TOOLS

This sounds straightforward, but it's important to have the right tools for **managing your project**. Tasks, reminders, and deadlines can being to pile up very quickly, and if you don't have your tools laid out at the start, it can be challenging to track your project's progress.

If you're working with the Rebus Community, you'll of course have access to the Rebus Community platform, designed to guide you through the open textbook publishing process and make it easy to find, recruit, and organize collaborators. The platform is a work in progress and new features are being released regularly, so keep an eye out! If you find that this platform doesn't do what you need it to, or would prefer to use another system, we've found Google Spreadsheets to be very helpful for keeping track of all the moving parts on a project.

It's also helpful to decide on **channels of communication** with your project team and leadership team. You can use the discussion option in the Rebus Community platform, Twitter, Slack, or email in any combination for day-to-day communication, and use video conferencing via Zoom, Skype, or Google Hangouts as needed. Take into account where your collaborators are located – if they are in different time zones than you are, an asynchronous mode of communication might be preferred. Other team members may also have varying access to fast or reliable internet, so video calls are not always the best option.

Lastly, you should also consider what **software** you will use for authoring, editing, formatting, and publishing your book. You could edit and revise your book in Google Docs, and use the Rebus Press (powered by Pressbooks) for formatting and publishing if you're working with us. Otherwise, you could work in other editing interfaces, such as Pages, MS Word, and with other formatting softwares, such as InDesign – but remember that these options don't always produce a range of formats, which can impact on how well a text can be accessed by students, and by others who wish to reuse & remix your content. Selecting your tools at the start lets you focus on refining content at every stage, instead having to make process decisions as you go.

PROJECT EXPECTATIONS

Open textbook or OER projects can quickly grow to become quite large as volunteers and collaborators see the potential impact of the book being created. It's important that you **reiterate your project's scope** to your team – what are you hoping to achieve in the first edition? What tasks and materials have already been set aside as future work? Whenever possible, **remind your team about the project's workload and timeline**. Letting others know that there is a clear plan of action towards publication will help allay stress and anxiety. And if needed, **revisit your project's timelines** so they are attainable, instead of just aspirational.

NEXT STEPS

Once you're ready and feel like you have a good grasp on your project, you can **start spreading the word**! As mentioned earlier, marketing is something that should be built into every stage of the publishing process, and promoting your project from the start will lay the groundwork for publicizing the book, finding collaborators, and encouraging adoptions in the future.

You can also **begin recruiting** editors, authors, or other volunteers as suits your project. Remember to welcome each new member to the community, introduce them to the team, and encourage them to share the news about the project!

Ready to get started on the next phase of publishing your book? We'll be working on guides for each stage of the publishing process, so stay tuned!

NEED FURTHER ASSISTANCE?

We hope these suggestions will help you lay the groundwork for your project and set it up for success from the beginning. We'll continue to add to this guide as we work with more projects, and we welcome your ideas on what else we could add, or your feedback on how these approaches have worked (or not!) for you.

If you have questions, or anything to add, please let us know in the Rebus Community project home.

 *This work is licensed under the Creative Commons Attribution 4.0 International License.*

Project Summary Template

This template may be used as you're starting to define your project. Find an editable version here.

PROJECT SUMMARY: [PROJECT TITLE]

Lead editor/author(s): [Name]

INTRODUCTION & ABOUT THE PROJECT

Welcome participants and potential volunteers. Explain how the project came about and why it is important/valuable to your discipline.

AUDIENCE

Identify both the primary student audience (academic level, discipline etc.) and any secondary audiences (instructors, researchers, professionals, other interested parties).

ABOUT THE TEXT/CONTENT

How will the text be structured? (e.g. 3 parts to every chapter, student-facing text plus instructor handbook etc.). What (if any) accompanying elements (e.g.

instructor resources, presentations, quizzes, maps, data sets) will be produced or collected?

LICENSING

Explain that the book will carry a CC-BY license and why. You may want to link to external resources where readers can go for more information on the CC BY license, such as the Creative Commons website, or the Rebus Community Licensing Policy.

Here is some optional copy that you can use to explain the nuances of including differently licensed materials within the same book: "While the global license for the book is CC-BY, some differently licensed materials may be included so long as they are clearly demarcated in the text and any changes are made in accordance with the conditions of the other license. This might apply in the cases of images, videos, or sections of non-CC-BY text that are essential to the book. However, we strongly discourage relying on this exception in order to protect and promote downstream uses. For more, see the [author guide]."

TEAM

Who is leading the project? Who else is involved? Provide contact details (not necessarily personal) and guidance on where to direct different kinds of queries.

SUPPORT (IF APPLICABLE)

Note any grants, institutional support or other external support the project has received or will receive over the course of the project.

TIMELINE

Provide an approximate timeline for the project. This doesn't have to be comprehensive, or rigid, but an indicator of dates for major milestones (e.g. chapters submitted, peer review complete, beta testing, initial release, etc.)

HOW TO GET INVOLVED

Offer clear guidance on how people can participate in the project, and where they should start (contact the project admin, comment on the forum, email someone, etc.). Consider making this general enough that you don't have to update it for different phases of the project. You may also want to link to other relevant resources you have, like author or review guides.

MEASURES OF SUCCESS

How will you know if you've met your goal? What constitutes success, and how will you measure it? Consider things like number of participants, diversity of perspectives (geographic, cultural, social, etc.), completed peer review process, number of adoptions etc. These don't have to be comprehensive, but help to clarify what success means to your project, beyond just writing a text.

Find an editable version of this template here.

CREATING & EDITING CONTENT

Authoring and Content Creation Summary

No single writing approach works for all projects. Instead, it will depend on the content creation team that you have in place and the type of resource you are trying to produce. This is an important time to pay attention to considerations such as accessibility, inclusion, tone, reading level, and other structural elements, which together will improve the overall quality of your content.

This summary covers the key issues in authoring and content creation, whether you're starting a new textbook or adapting an existing resource.

<table>
<tr><td align="center">Underlying principles</td></tr>
<tr><td>

Always keep the audience front of mind. Authors should have a clear understanding of the book's eventual readers, why it is being created, what needs it fills, and how to keep the content culturally relevant.

Get support from others. Create pathways for authors to work with and get input from instructional designers, potential adopters, and students, so the finished book is effective and valuable.

Model good practices. Use your author guide and model chapter to show authors how to incorporate accessibility, structure content in modules (for potential adapters), track glossary terms, properly tag key concepts, and enter citations.

</td></tr>
</table>

Remember that creation can be iterative. Content can be expanded on, revised, and improved over time: the first release doesn't need to include everything. Start with the core concepts, and then add case studies, media, quizzes, assignments, question banks, and slide decks.

Who's Involved?

We suggest three options for creating content: sole authoring, small-team collaboration, or large-team sharing. All three options have advantages and challenges, as below:

- Sole authoring: clearest understanding of work and content; minimal logistical administration; no shared workload; strong need for external feedback and multiple perspectives

- Small team: needs shared vision, shared ownership; some administration and coordination required; workload is shared; perspectives are diverse but additional feedback from reviewers can enhance content; changes to team can have a big impact; small but active community around resource

- Large team: needs greatest buy-in to shared vision, clear schedule, and timeline; most administration and coordination; documentation required; workload is shared; needs champions to maintain team motivation; many perspectives, requiring copyeditors and reviewers to ensure consistency and cohesiveness; largest community around your resource

Key Tactics

Putting in planning and decision-making time up front is one of the most important things to do. This is true whether you are a single author or part of a writing team.

- Create a detailed outline, in consultation with instructional designers, that lays out a clear structure or skeleton for the resource.
- Using the outline, identify potential areas of overlap so as to reduce the need for substantive editing down the road.
- Prepare an author guide with:

  - style guide
  - chapter template
  - model chapter
  - licensing information
  - author expectations (about accessibility & inclusive design, non-textual elements, modular content)
  - details on writing tools
  - submission and contact information

- Keep a tracking sheet so you know the status of your content creation.
- Stay in constant communication with your team – for introductions, outline discussions, unit assessments, deadline adjustments, etc.
- Conduct author calls and post updates/recaps on the public project home page.
- Build a list of FAQs to share with existing and new team members.
- Be clear about the timing and process of next steps, including editing, proofreading, review, formatting, etc.

Authors should get out of the project as much as they put in, so do what you can to reward them, recognize their efforts, and make their experience a good one! This will leave you with a happy and vibrant community around your resource, which will also be reflected in the final product.

Read on to learn more about creating content for your open textbook.

Authoring and Content Creation Overview

This section of *The Rebus Guide to Publishing Open Textbooks (So Far)* is designed to help you with one of the biggest parts of your project – creating the content! This section will run through everything you need to keep in mind while authoring the book, creating ancillary materials (slide decks, question banks, assignments, sidebars, workbooks, etc.), adapting a book, and more. It is licensed under a Creative Commons Attribution 4.0 International License (CC BY) and you are welcome to print this document, make a copy for yourself, or share with others.

Read through the sections below, and consider the suggestions as you begin writing or creating the content of your book. These sections are also intended for anyone who is adapting a book, or remixing multiple resources. If you have any questions about the guide, please feel free to post them in the Rebus Community project home. This document is an evolving draft, based on our experience managing open textbook projects and community feedback. We welcome your thoughts and contributions, so let us know how it works for you, or if you have any suggestions to improve the guide.

GOING SOLO VS. WORKING AS A TEAM

Before we dive into the nitty-gritty of creating content, let's first take a look at the people behind the work. No two projects will take the same approach, and as such, the process of creating content will always be very different. In general, though, there are three options: one author creates all the content, a small team share the work, or a larger group of authors split it into smaller pieces. Each of these approaches has advantages and disadvantages, so if you're trying to decide on the best option for you, or want to know what to expect, read on! We'll use the example of writing the main text of the book here, but the same can apply to any other kind of content.

If you're taking on the challenge as the only author, the resource is, of course, entirely your own work, and you will know it inside and out. This makes it easy for you to keep track of what is happening in different parts of the book, avoiding duplication or conflicts, and maintaining consistency in structure, tone, etc. In addition, there's almost no external wrangling or organising to worry about (yay!). However, writing a lot of content on your own is a big job. Staying motivated and on track without a team around you can be difficult, but ultimately you know better than anyone what you're able to manage. If you are the only author on a text, keep in mind you will need to rely on peer review for feedback and different perspectives or expertise, as it's your main chance to get other eyes on the content, so be sure to give good guidelines to your reviewers so you can get the specific kinds of feedback you need, along with anything else they see fit to highlight.

Small teams operate slightly differently than solo authors. If you're part of a small team, keep in mind that most importantly, you will need a shared vision of the resource, and a clear schedule to help drive creation and ensure a cohesive end product. A team can develop a clear sense of shared ownership over the project, without the same level of work needed if you were to go it alone, but it takes some effort to keep everyone on the same page. In addition, small teams will also hopefully contain a few different perspectives which can, together, shape what content looks like. However, since you are all still a small pool, and very close to the content, you will benefit from the input of external reviewers. Lastly, small teams do require some organizing and coordination throughout the process that needs to be managed carefully and it should be noted that one person dropping out or failing to meet their commitments can have a big effect on the other members of the team.

If you're part of a large team, you will also require a shared vision and a clear schedule and timeline. Large teams will require more organising, wrangling, and documentation to get started and keep on track – and a good leadership team is critical. However, the workload on such teams is much more manageable for each author, as content can be broken down into as many pieces as desired. Large teams will benefit from having a champion (or two or three) who is keeping spirits high and motivating the team to keep going, and as a whole, it tends to be easier to pick up the slack if any members drop out. Large teams are potentially full of interesting, original and diverse perspectives, which can have a wonderful impact on content, but review becomes critical for ensuring consistency and cohesiveness, as well as accuracy. Overall, the experience can take some work for the organisers, but it can be an excellent opportunity for everyone involved to grow their networks, form a vibrant community around the resource and ensure its long term success.

Choosing between these approaches really depends on the type and structure of the content you are creating, your vision for the resource, your expertise, and your capacity to commit to writing. Any one of them can be successful, and keep in mind that you can adjust to bring on more authors if you find that a one-person effort or small team is proving challenging.

PROCESS

Whatever the makeup of your writing team, putting in time to plan out your content and make some key decisions up front is the single-most important thing you can do. Approaching writing with the right foundation will make not only the writing process easier, but also editing and reviewing down the line. This section is written mostly with team organising in mind, but a solo author can still pull out some useful information on preparing for and managing the writing process. If you're planning to work with a team of authors but haven't yet assembled them, check out our recruitment guide first.

If you already have your **authoring team assembled**, one of the first steps is to **start working on a detailed outline**. You can approach this collaboratively, as a team or with each author working on their own chapter, or the lead author may set the framework themselves. In any case, be sure to solicit input from everyone involved to see if there are any gaps or additions that they would make. This process is vital to lay out a clear structure or skeleton of the resource, that can be filled in over the course of the writing/creation stage, and everyone on the authoring team should know it inside and out.

Creating or reviewing an outline together can also help to **identify potential areas of overlap** between chapters, or complementary sections, allowing authors to write with an eye to the larger text as they go, which will help reduce the need for substantial editing down the road. In addition, be sure to think clearly about the goals and final use of the resource established during the project scoping phase, and its positioning relative to existing materials or resources – this may lead you to structure things differently, address areas that are commonly excluded from or underrepresented in existing texts, or help you to make sure you cover the core areas of interest.

With the outline in hand, you can also **prepare an author guide**. This is another central tool to ensure shared understanding and consistency, and can include a **style guide**, **chapter template**, **model chapter**, as well as information about **writing tools, licensing, accessibility, media, author expectations, submission information**, and **contact details** for the lead author or project manager. Check out our author guide template for some guidance if you need it – it includes all these elements which you can to adapt to fit your project. We've also collected a few examples of author guides used in some of our open textbook projects so you can see the different approaches people have taken: *Introduction to Philosophy*, *History of Science and Technology*, and *Introduction to North American Archaeology*. Overall, the author guide is an important part of making sure the content created is coherent and consistent, even if it's written by a range of people, and to ensure that all these authors have the information they need to do their best work!

As the project manager or content coordinator, you should also put together a **simple tracking sheet** to keep an eye on status of each piece of content. Having this information collected in one document will save you the time and mental frustration of looking through emails, chats, or other conversations with authors for an update. We've prepared a content tracking template that you can copy and adapt for your project as needed.

Next, make sure you **share these documents with the authors**, and use this opportunity to **conduct an author call** and **introduce various members of the team** with one another. If your team is spread across different time zones, you could instead share the information on a public discussion forum, email, or using whatever agreed upon methods of communication suit your project. **Relay information** about **deadlines**, **expectations**, and **process** with the authors, address any questions that come up, and incorporate any other information authors identify as being useful to them. Then, it's time to let them write!

It's good to give authors the space they need to make content, but at the same time, it can be a solitary process and it's good to make sure that they don't feel isolated from the rest of the team and any other progress being made. **Ongoing collaboration and communication** between authors and the team will help, and it can also provide some gentle nudging to help keep people on track. It's also good to be able to course-correct as you go, rather than only catching issues or confusion later in the process. If possible, **conduct regular check-ins and author calls**, and if authors contact you with any questions over the course of this period, **start building a list of FAQs** to share with the team.

Lastly, once you're **collecting content** that has been drafted or is ready for the next stage, thank the author for their time and **provide clear details regarding the next steps** in the process so they know what happens next. If the author's involvement will be needed down the line (e.g. to implement revisions after editing and peer review), let them know now so this work doesn't come as a surprise later. Now's also your chance to make sure you can to keep the author engaged going forward, by providing project updates or more (see our engagement guide for ideas). Authors can become great champions and even adopters for your project in future!

CONSIDERATIONS WHEN CREATING CONTENT

While authors are subject matter experts, creating quality educational resources requires other skills and considerations that should, again, be given some thought up front. The following is not an exhaustive list, but should help prompt you as you're entering and navigating the creation phase.

1. AUDIENCE

First of all, the most important thing to keep in mind when creating content are the **learners and instructors** who will be using the book. Authors should have a clear sense of **who the resources is for, why it is being created, what need it fills in the field, and how best to keep it culturally relevant**. These details should be kept front of mind throughout the entire creation process to help shape and strengthen the text – for instance, through learning outcomes clearly presented at the start of each chapter or section, or examples in the book that ensure that all students will see themselves reflected or represented in the text.

To help with this, you should also, if you can, draw on support from your campus or faculty's **instructional design team** who can help you find the best ways to deliver content to students. This perspective should be included from early on to avoid the need for retroactive changes, and so that the end result is an effective and valuable teaching resource.

2. ACCESSIBILITY AND INCLUSIVE DESIGN

In a similar vein, it's important that you think of *all* learners when creating your content, which means making sure it is released as an accessible resource that doesn't require much, if any, remediation to meet the needs of the students using it. We believe very strongly in building **accessibility** into content from day one, not only in terms of **technical accessibility**, but also **language** and **inclusive design** [1]. It's also worth remembering that

1. **Note:** According to the Inclusive Design Research Centre (IDRC) at The Ontario College of Art and Design University, inclusive design is "design that considers the full range of human diversity with respect to ability, language, culture, gender, age and other forms

designing for the margins is, well, just good design! It's remarkable how many best practices for accessibility make the text better for everybody reading it (e.g. clear hierarchy & structure, captions on videos, etc.), as well as the obvious benefit of supporting students with recognised disabilities.

Again, try to reach out to accessibility and inclusive design teams or instructional designers (as mentioned in the previous section) on your campus for support if you can, so that you can incorporate good design practices into your book that benefit all students. Here are a few of the kinds of things you can do to improve your resource's accessibility in the writing phase:

- use heading styles in your documents to create a consistent hierarchy
- consider reading levels of the audience and adjust your tone accordingly
- state the full-forms of acronyms during their first use in each chapter
- include alt. text for functional images
- use appropriate and clear link text (don't link words like "here", "there," etc.)
- prepare clear tables with appropriate header information, captions, and more

For more information and guidance on creating an accessible open resource, we highly recommend the *BCcampus Open Education Accessibility Toolkit*. We've also included a short list of basic considerations in our author guide template.

3. BUILD FOR ADAPTABILITY

Shifting focus slightly to the **instructors** who will be using the resource, wherever possible, we encourage you to create content that is easily

of human difference." Like the IDRC, we use the term inclusive design as opposed to universal design deliberately – see the section titled "Why not use the term Universal Design?" on the IDRC's website for more.

adaptable and modular. One of the major goals of any educational resource is to encourage a wide use, and a major advantage of openly licensed resources is that they can also be adapted and localised by those users. Take some time to consider the changes that other instructors may want to make as they set out to use your resource in their courses, and do what you can to make it easy for changes to take place. One way to do this is to **keep context specific examples in blocks** that can be swapped out for localised content (e.g. discussion of national policies, course, or institution specific information, etc.). Another way is to **be clear about licenses and attributions** of different elements in the resource (images, excerpts, videos, etc.) so that future users will not need to spend added time looking these up. This is especially important in the case of anything that has been included with a one-time permission or relying on fair-use, and including a back matter section with this kind of information is one way to make it clear to future adapters.

4. THINK AHEAD

With a bit of foresight, there are a few tasks you can simplify by laying the groundwork while you write. For example, identifying and tracking where glossary or index terms appear as you write can be much easier than trying to locate them all at the end! Other examples of this kind of forethought we've seen include keeping track of the citations/references in each chapter for a bibliography, tagging key concepts using HTML classes to make it easy to format them consistently with CSS, or keeping a spreadsheet to track images and other media to simplify licensing checks. Knowing what appears where in your book is always useful, and the more you can do along the way, the easier life will be in the long run!

5. CREATION CAN BE ITERATIVE

We also encourage taking the approach that **creation can be iterative**, meaning that content can be expanded on, revised, and improved over time. The first release doesn't need to contain everything you want to include in the long run, so you could, for example, release the core theory sections of each chapter, then expand over time with case studies, media elements, quizzes, in-class assignments, or other ancillaries. Alternatively, if your text has clearly defined sections, you could work on these one at a time, releasing them as you go. This helps to give a sense of progress (both to yourself and others), and can be a great way to encourage others to get involved – seeing the text coming together is often the best way for people to understand the project and see how they can contribute. And, with OER, releasing content is in some ways just the beginning! Other versions can emerge through the work of others that may then feed back into the original.

6. MAKE THE EXPERIENCE REWARDING

Lastly, as a project manager or lead author, think carefully about what your authors (and you!) get out of this process. Authors should get out of the project as much as they put in, so do what you can to reward them, recognize their efforts, and make their experience on the project a good one! Ensuring that you do so will not only leave you with a happy team and community around your resource, but will also reflect in the final product. For more on how to manage and reward authors, see our volunteer management guide.

7. MODEL GOOD PRACTICES

As you might imagine, ensuring these approaches are embedded in the creation process is a little more tricky when working with a team, which is where a good author guide is critical. In addition, you can **prepare a model chapter** that you can share with authors that lays out the various elements and formatting. You can use the author guide to surface particular points about your audience, share best practices for writing with accessibility in mind, and use the model chapter as an example of the tone, format, and structure a chapter should take. Doing so will make it clearer for authors how they can do their part, which also helps to reduce the amount of work needed in the editorial or formatting phases.

NEED FURTHER ASSISTANCE?

We hope these suggestions will help you plan and oversee the authoring and creation phase of your project. We'll continue to add to this guide as we work with more projects, and we welcome your ideas on what else we could add, or your feedback on how these approaches have worked (or not!) for you.

If you have questions, or anything to add, please let us know in the Rebus Community project home.

Author Guide Template

This template may be used as you are welcoming new authors on your project. Find an editable version here.

AUTHOR GUIDE: [PROJECT TITLE]

Lead editor(s)/author(s): [Name(s)]

[Link to Project Homepage]

OVERVIEW

This section can be adapted from (or link to) the Project Summary. Be sure to specify the license of the OER and any contributions made.

AUTHOR COMMITMENTS

Introduce the existing authors and state the expected qualifications & expertise of any contributing authors.

CONTENT GUIDELINES

Course & Audience Information

Provide key details about the course and identify your student audience.

Student Learning Outcomes

Provide a list of student learning outcomes mapped to which chapters they will be covered in. This will serve as a quick reference point to ensure proper scaffolding across the resource.

Structure

Explain the structure of each section/chapter (e.g. each chapter comprises a background/theory chapter, a case study and a student workbook section). Provide word count ranges to ensure expectations are met.

Citation Style

Citations should follow the [MLA/APA/Chicago etc.] style. References to historical figures should include the dates of birth and death in parentheses, such as: Karl Marx (1813-1883). The text as a whole will be edited in accordance with the [Chicago Manual of Style].

Accessibility

Authors are asked to ensure that their sections fulfill accessibility best practices. Building in certain key elements from the beginning will make a big difference in ensuring the text is accessible to all students who will use it in their courses. The following are the main areas to keep in mind — follow the links to read more.

Organization of content/Headings — Many students need clear cues to navigate content, so keeping the organisation and hierarchy consistent are important. Use heading styles from the style menu rather than bold, italic or different font sizes to indicate the start of a new section. This helps to structure the content in a logical way for all students, including those using screen readers.

Lists — Make sure you use the standardized numbered and bulleted lists found on the style menu, rather than plain text. E.g.:

1. Numbered
2. List

- Bulleted
- List

Images & colour — Include a text description for any functional images that communicate important information. This will likely be more in depth than an image caption, and should contain enough information that a student can understand the concept depicted without seeing the image. (Note: this isn't required for decorative images!). You should also avoid using colour as the only means of communicating information (e.g. on a graph).

Tables — Make sure you avoid inserting images of tables, and instead enter the content as an editable table. This ensures that it will be accessible for students using screen readers.

Multimedia — If you're including video or audio content, it should ideally have captions or a transcript available. If this is not available for a resource in your section, please flag this in your submission for the editing team to address.

The information above is drawn from the BCcampus Open Education Accessibility Toolkit. Please read through the rest of the text for more on accessibility best practices.

Media (Images, Video, Audio etc.)

Note any requested or required media that the author should supply, and the preferred formats (if any). You can also offer sources where authors may find appropriately licensed content, e.g.:

Where appropriate, you can choose to include images, video or sound clips along with the written text. Please ensure that these elements are in the public domain or carry a CC-BY, CC-BY-SA or a CC0 license, and that you clearly indicate and link to the source in your submission.

The following are useful sources of public domain and CC-BY licensed multimedia content:

- The Internet Archive
- Creative Commons
- The Met Museum
- Flickr
- Open Culture
- Free Music Archive
- Pixabay
- Pexels
- Wikimedia Commons

Note that all images should be given captions and descriptive alternative text, where appropriate.

Glossary

If applicable, indicate to authors how to highlight and define glossary terms. You may want to avoid using styles like italics/bold/underline to display glossary terms in-text, as this may not be distinguishable enough from the main text. We recommend asking authors to highlight glossary terms in a bright colour so they are clearly identifiable.

SUBMISSION INFORMATION

Due Dates

Indicate either a specific due date for content submission (if it will be the same for all contributors), or note that this will be arranged between the editors and authors and give an estimated timeframe (e.g. 6 weeks). A target date for having all content submitted may also be helpful, and links to any project tracking spreadsheets should be provided here.

How to Submit

Instruct contributors on how they should submit their sections once completed. This should include format (generally Word or Google Doc), method (email attachment, add to shared Google Drive etc.), contact person and indication that they will be notified when the submission has been received.

Editing & Review

This section should give a broad outline of the editing & review process a contributor's section will go through once it has been received. It doesn't need to be very detailed, but should give the author an idea of what to expect (e.g. the lead editor will leave comments for the author to address, then the content will go through an anonymous peer review process). We also encourage project leads to involve authors in deciding what the editing and review process will look like, which can be indicated in this section.

Recognition for Contributors

Include details about compensation and recognition for contributors, such as: "This project couldn't happen without your participation. All contributing authors will be credited prominently in their chapter, the book and promotional materials. All editors, reviewers and other contributors will also be credited."

Editing Summary

Editing encompasses many different processes that help make your book into a whole, cohesive resource that fulfils its intended learning objectives. It takes place at the broad scale and at the granular level, as well as many stages in between.

This summary outlines how editing provides structure, appeal, and nuance to your resource, making it more understandable and easy to read.

<table>
<tr><td>Underlying principles</td></tr>
<tr><td>

Don't let great be the enemy of good. Editing and revisions will always expand to fill the time allotted to it. At a certain point, you need to stop and be satisfied with your content, rather than trying to make everything 'perfect.'

Make the text work better for its readers. Ensure that your editors keep accessibility, reading levels, and format in mind, so that everybody reading the book can find value in it.

Keep an eye on the clock. Timing is key, whether you want to reach strategic deadlines, stop yourself from over-editing, or seamlessly hand off content from one person to the next. Always watch your schedules, even if they were only best estimates, but be willing to tweak them as needed.

Roles are not written in stone. Editors can serve multiple roles, as well as provide informal feedback, act as generalist reviewers, do beta-testing, or help with formatting.

</td></tr>
</table>

Who's Involved?

Editing can take place at many points during the book's production, with different kinds of editors involved at each stage:

- Project managers, acting as managing editors, shape the resource as a whole, throughout the course of the project

- Content editors focus on what should be included and excluded from the book, acting as hands-on subject-matter experts

- Developmental (or structural) editors focus on how that content comes together, shaping the book's structure so as to meet learning objectives. They need not be subject-matter experts

- Substantive editors are ideally subject-matter experts, and do a lot of work related to resolving questions and issues, and addressing areas of improvement (as identified by the developmental editor)

- Copyeditors work at the granular level, closely reading and editing for sentence structure, grammar, syntax, vocabulary, voice, and punctuation. They may also assist with permissions, citations, layout, and design details during the book's formatting

- Proofreaders perform the final inspection and make small corrections to spelling and punctuation

Key Tactics

Creating a positive experience for editors relies on setting out clear expectations, structured tools, and simple guidelines:

- Prepare a style guide that covers citation styles, formatting (general and specialized, like for glossaries), spelling, accessibility, etc.

- Make sure editors are aware of their roles, deadlines, and communications tools by setting up an editorial workflow and being transparent as things progress.

- Build a sense of teamwork by connecting your editors with authors, instructional designers, and other collaborators, while encouraging open dialogue among them.

- As needed, ask editors to pay attention to specific tasks, such as formatting, checking permissions and rights, gathering feedback from reviewers and testers, etc.

- Make sure content has been copyedited before peer review, so reviewers are more focused when it comes to providing feedback.

- Ask editors to provide positive feedback about well-executed or clearly explained concepts (rather than solely identifying areas that need improvement).

- If possible, find a budget to pay editors, especially a developmental editor and copyeditor.

Ultimately, the goals of your open textbook project will shape the editing needs, and you may need to keep a firm hand on things. It's all in service of making the book a more usable and productive resource!

Read on to learn more about editing content in your open textbook.

Editing Overview

This section of *The Rebus Guide to Publishing Open Textbooks (So Far)* is intended to help you throughout the various phases of editing that go into creating your open textbook. It runs through everything you need to keep in mind while working on the book's content or ancillary materials (slide decks, question banks, assignments, sidebars, workbooks, etc.) It is licensed under a Creative Commons Attribution 4.0 International License (CC BY) and you are welcome to print this document, make a copy for yourself, or share with others.

In what follows, consider our guidelines as you are creating a new open textbook, adapting an existing book, or remixing multiple resources – editing is critical to each of these projects, but might surface in different ways. Depending on your project, certain editorial functions may be more relevant as you start working on your book's outline (with project managers as editors), later during writing and review (involving content, structural, developmental, and copy editors), or even towards the time when you are closer to formatting (when proofreaders and others take a final look). We'll go through each of these functions and roles below, so keep reading! If you have any questions about the guide, please post them in the Rebus Community project home. The *Guide* is an evolving document, based on our experience managing open textbook projects and from giving and receiving (much) community feedback. We welcome your thoughts and contributions, so let us know how it works for you, or if you have any suggestions to improve the *Guide*.

Special thanks to Elizabeth Mays for her contributions to this overview – Liz is the former marketing manager for Rebus and current director of sales and marketing for Pressbooks, as well as adjunct faculty member at Arizona State University, and author and editor of two open textbooks (*Media Innovation and Entrepreneurship* and *A Guide to Making Open Textbooks with Students*)!

WHY DOES EDITING MATTER?

Editing is one of the most crucial phases in creating an OER, equally or perhaps even more important than writing itself! Editing allows the chapters/units, sections, and subsections to come together as a whole, cohesive textbook. It creates throughlines and connections between the book's themes, and makes the reading experience smoother and more productive for learners. Some editors say that editing is "the process of finding patterns" in a piece of writing—either at the macro level of the trajectory of the whole work, or at the micro level of grammar and syntax. In between those extremes, editing helps smooth out the edges and makes the text more useable. You might say that writing puts together the raw material of a textbook, while editing focuses on providing structure, appeal, and nuance. Editing makes content easier to read.

It's also important to know that editing is really an umbrella term for a lot of different processes. It can be useful to think of editing in terms of scale, with different editors performing different tasks at the beginning, middle, and end of the project. Editing starts with the big picture, like the subject of the book and how it is treated, as well as the broader discourse of which the book will be a part. It then narrows in on mid-range aspects, such as how the chapters are ordered and structured, and what themes will be included or left out. Usually (though not always), the editing that takes place later on gets down to more granular details, including fact-checking and spelling and punctuation. Remembering to keep the different scales of editing in mind throughout the project is good if you're aiming at creating a well-rounded resource. Through this approach, editing ensures that the content fits the purpose, and fulfils the learning objectives that you set out for the resource during project scoping.

Editing is also a valuable way to have many different pairs of eyes on the content throughout various stages of creation, from conception and first drafts through formatting, proofreading, and the final versions before release. Along the way, editors will make everything from substantial to incremental revisions, improving the overall quality, readability, and relevancy. In this manner, editing also functions as a kind of review, where people who are not necessarily subject-matter experts read through and adjust the content. Editing as review is an important aspect of this process, and a useful source of critique, feedback, and suggestions that will ultimately improve the resource.

THE DIFFERENT KINDS OF EDITING, AND WHO DOES THEM

As mentioned at the start of this section, editing can take place during all phases of the project, as early as project scoping, and as late as final formatting. Below, we go into the different types of editing that are common to open textbook projects, including who might be best to take on these tasks.

Project management (as editing)

Let's start with a role that may not seem like a typical editorial function: the project manager. The project manager is responsible for running the process of creating a resource from start to release (and often after). In this respect, it is a role very similar to the managing editor in a conventional publishing house. In collaboration with the other editors and leadership team, the project manager thinks about the resource as a whole, and identifies patterns that allow it to fit in with (or stand out from) other books or resources in the field. The project manager shapes not just the book, but the project as a whole, including who participates and how things unroll over time. The project manager assures that the final resource meets the needs set out at the start of the project, while helping develop style guides, chapter templates, author guides, etc., and how they are followed (or revised) over time.

Content editing (subject-matter editing)

Content editing, also known as subject-matter editing, takes place at a somewhat more detailed scale than project management, but still takes a broad perspective on the book as a whole. It is a function that more often comes to mind when we hear the word "editor." Content editing includes decisions about what will be included and excluded from a given book, as well as soliciting and synthesizing feedback about the content from the community of potential contributors and users. It is conducted by someone with subject-matter expertise in the field at hand, as well as perspectives on what is currently missing within that field and/or how it could grow. Ultimately, the content editor is largely responsible for moulding and shaping the book, and does so in a fairly hands-on manner, focusing on "what should be said." Content editors often work closely with authors until they are satisfied that all the content has been appropriately covered. They may also serve as a go-between, communicating the leadership team's vision to those who are producing the words that speak to that vision.

Developmental editing (structural editing)

Developmental editing is often referred to as structural editing, and the latter name suggests, it focuses on the structure of your textbook. (The first unit of Open Textbook Network's Publishing Curriculum is dedicated to dissecting just this, and it is worth checking out!) Whereas content editing focuses on the **what**, developmental editing addresses the **how**. Developmental editors need not be subject-matter experts, and in fact are often more effective when they come at the material from a distance. Without that "expert lens" on the content, they may be more able focus on "how it should be said." This type of editing is all about making sure the textbook is set up to meet learning objectives, and in so doing, that students are set up to succeed.

Substantive editing

The substantive editor often involves both creativity and a certain amount of heavy-lifting. These processes include resolving many of the questions, problems, and needed improvements about content that are identified during the developmental edit. The substantive edit refers to structural revisions that happen at the chapter level as well as writing revisions that take place, line-by-line, at the paragraph level. In this phase, an editor may take the liberty of reorganizing sections, recasting sentences, and making queries and recommendations (either for the writers or other editors on the project). Since the substantive editor makes changes to the content itself, ideally they should be a subject-matter expert, or have a strong familiarity with the book's content. If they are not experienced in the subject, the substantive editor should work closely with the content editor or lead author, and be sure not to make changes that might alter the meaning or accuracy of the text.

Copyediting

The copyeditor does very close reading of the text, making corrections to sentence structure, grammar, syntax issues, vocabulary, and punctuation. At this phase of the of the process, they are less focused on the bigger picture, but may in some cases rewrite sentences or adjust language details. If so, it should be with the goal of serving the editorial objectives of the book as a whole, or in order to maintain consistency with other sections and chapters.

Usually, the copyeditor also does a certain amount of "style editing" or "mechanical editing," which ensures the book meets the tone and style that has been determined during earlier phases of the project. This may also be necessary to ensure that the "voice" is internally consistent throughout. In some cases, a copyeditor will check layout and design details, such as figure numbers, headers, citations, and other elements, once a book is formatted. A copyeditor may also be responsible for checking permissions on images, media, quotes, excerpts, and other elements in your book.

Proofreading

Often combined (or confused) with copyediting, proofreading is a distinct process that involves fine adjustments at the scale of spelling and punctuation errors, formatting issues, or other non–content-specific aspects of the book. The proofreader goes through the book from start to finish as a final check before (and sometimes after) formatting. You can think of proofreading as a final inspection, ensuring everything is polished and properly lined up. Ideally the proofreader is someone with a fresh eye, who has not already been involved in editing, and therefore does not already know the manuscript well. Proofreaders don't need to have subject-matter expertise: their experience of reading the book may well be very similar to new students or readers. As such, their feedback on the book overall is invaluable! Occasionally the proofreader may also function as the copyeditor, but we always recommend two separate pairs of eyes for these roles when possible. Having someone do a final read of the book once all the edits and revisions have been made is very valuable.

WHEN DOES EACH KIND OF EDITING TAKE PLACE?

In addition to the **what** and **how** mentioned above, it's good to keep in mind the **when** of different types of editing. This helps you plan your project timeline, and account for the work that each stage of editing takes, ultimately allowing you to stay on schedule., The order of editing processes usually follows the outline above—from bigger scale to smaller—and as usual, we find that the more you do upfront, the better. However, you may find that all chapters follow their own timeline to a certain extent, and from week to week may be at different stages of editing. Factors like the timing of what has already been written, what resources you have available, and what holdups arise will all affect the editing process.

Before jumping into the details, here are a few general pointers:

- Don't let great be the enemy of good. By this, we mean that editing will always expand to fill the time that is allotted for it. At a certain point, you need to stop and not try to make things "perfect" (which doesn't exist, in any case!) If you allocate six weeks for the developmental edit, keep to that deadline, and stop work when you get there. Improvements can take place informally down the line, so flag outstanding issues during the official time frame, and deal with them on an ongoing basis.

- Underpromise and overdeliver – on deadlines, that is. Always assume that tasks will run over time, so be strategic when scheduling. If you have six weeks for the developmental edit, tell your editor that their deadline is in four weeks. If they do require a two-week extension eventually, you will have minimized any flow-on effects that delay things down the line.

- Revisions can be a seemingly never-ending cycle. Think carefully about how many times you want content to go back and forth between authors and editors. Not only does it affect timelines, but it can also put more pressure on your authors than you had intended. If in doubt, ask authors their preference!

- Timing is key for all editing processes, but in the case of copyediting it has particular implications for the peer-review phase. If a text is not copyedited before peer review, it can affect what the reviewers focus on and what kind of value they provide to the project. For instance, a reviewer can become frustrated by or be overly attentive to issues of style, grammar, and punctuation, and that is not how their expertise is best used. We recommend doing as much editing as possible before review, so that reviewers can focus solely on content and other components listed in your review guide. However, if you don't have the time or resources for this, request your content and developmental editors to keep an eye out for glaring issues relating to grammar and readability and inform your peer reviewers in advance that the text has not been copyedited. That way you can either ask them to focus on big-picture issues and ignore the more granular ones.

We've divvied up the editing tasks throughout the publishing process below and included some approximations of how long these might take, so take a look and let us know if your experience differs, Estimating timelines is always a best guess (and of course differs from project to project), but the more examples we gather, the more we can keep refining these estimates. The numbers below are based on a book of seven chapters, with 3,000 words each.

Editing before writing

A portion of developmental editing can actually take place before content is written, as part of the project scoping process. Content and developmental editors can work together to help prepare the book's outline, style guide, chapter template, author guide, concept maps, and more. We expect this kind of work to take approximately two to four weeks.

Editing after writing

Once your texts are largely written, you can expect content editing to take about four to five hours per chapter. The developmental edit, might then take roughly seven weeks for the full book (approximately a week per chapter). This is followed by the substantive edit, entailing three to four weeks for the complete text.

Editing after revisions

Following the content, developmental, and substantive revisions, the chapters should be in a good state to go to the copyeditor. We suggest allocating two to four weeks for copyediting. Once it is done, you should be ready to send the content out to peer reviewers. And if you don't have the time or resources for a comprehensive copyedit before review, we suggest getting your content and developmental editors to resolve any glaring grammatical errors that affect the readability of the text during their edits, so the content is reasonably easy for reviewers to parse through. In lieu of this, we recommend informing reviewers if the content has not been copyedited, and in some cases, may be able to request them to take a light pass over content during their review.

Editing after review and revisions

If the peer-review process brings forward any recommendations for changes (which it almost surely will), an additional round of revisions will be required, including possibly a light copyedit. Following that, the book will be ready for formatting, which then leads to proofreading. Depending on how "clean" the text is, the proofreader might take approximately two weeks. Hopefully, seeing that the book has by now been through multiple rounds of edits and revisions, this last phase is all about catching small errors and formatting details.

OTHER CONSIDERATIONS WHILE EDITING

As we've said before, creating high-quality educational resources entails more than just writing accurate content. Several other considerations should be given thought up front, to ensure that your content can be read with a critical eye, while also serving the broader needs of open and inclusive education. The following is not an exhaustive list, but should help prompt you as you're entering and navigating the editing phase.

Accessibility

It's important to keep all learners in mind when working to create your resource. One of the best ways to avoid the need for excessive remediation once a textbook is released is to keep accessibility in mind during editing. Many principles of good design, technical accessibility, and language covered are in our authoring overview. These apply during the editing phase as well: try to use this time to check to see if you're meeting best practices regarding accessibility (e.g., clear hierarchy and structure, captions on videos, alt text on images, plain language, etc.). Editing is about making the text work better for its readers—this means everybody reading it, including not only students with recognized disabilities, but all those with varying learning or language abilities. Make sure all editors understand that they have a role in this, and provide them with the guidance resources they need if they are not already aware of the specific issues at stake.

Audience and Reading Level

In a similar vein to accessibility, we recommend that all editors keep in mind the reading level of the book's audience, as well as the learning objectives that it is supposed to meet. There are a number of online tools that perform readability checks on content, such as *Hemingway Editor*, but we also recommend speaking to instructional designers and librarians at your institution for standards and resources best suited to your context. With this information, editors can understand how reading levels affect their context, and help the content fit the best standards for target readers.

Rights and Permissions

Checking permissions on images, excerpts, and other media in your book is a team effort. The project manager or section leads can identify open repositories to source these elements, while authors can do an initial check when including external content in their contributions. When it comes to confirming permissions, the editor assigned to a given section can more easily conducts a final check. This type of work is sometimes best done when going through the book line by line, so if your team does not have a member dedicated to rights and permissions, then the copyeditor can take this on, in line with their fact checking duties.

Formatting and Review

During the course of their work, an editor may serve as a de facto formatter and/or reviewer. Content corrections, such as to headings, images, or captions can assist with the book's formatting. As well, formal or casual feedback from editors (including proofreaders) can be taken as a non-peer, "generalist" review, which provides a student-like perspective, or someone else who is reading the book for the first time. Editors also provide benefit by thinking about the text as a whole, providing invaluable feedback in a way that a reviewer of a single chapter might not be able to.

We're all human, and that means authors too!

As you work to improve your resource, try to be reasonable about the number of revisions or edits that you ask of your authors. While some are happy to continue redrafting many times over, others might not be as willing or have other demands on their time. It is best to set expectations up front, be transparent as things progress, and carefully gauge how your authors react when you ask them for a second, third, or fourth revision. Tread carefully – writers are only human!

There are practical considerations to being gentle with them, too. Your role as an editor is two-fold: offering critiques to structure and content to help make resource stronger, while recognizing (and crediting) well-executed and clearly explained concepts and ideas to make your authors stronger. By telling them when something works well, it reinforces the models you want to see throughout the draft. Be nice in your comments and suggestions, and start with the positive aspects of what has been written—you want to be sure that the 'good' is preserved during the process of revising the less-good. Highlight both the positive and the issues in each draft, because it eventually creates a dialogue with your authors, while supporting the positive environment that will allow everyone to work on improving the book.

If you have the budget, hire some help!

Although these editorial guidelines are generally true for most textbooks, every project differs. If yours includes funding to pay freelance editors, it can be worth the outlay in order to gain the "baked-in" expertise that comes with a professional developmental or substantive editor, copyeditor or proofreader. Many freelancers double as subject-matter experts, and can act as advisors or coaches to your volunteer editors, throughout the process, including input during the project scoping and outline creation stages. See our section on hiring outside editors for more details and considerations (coming soon!).

REBUS' EXPERIENCE WITH EDITING OPEN TEXTBOOK PROJECTS

Over time, we keep being reminded that open textbook projects are never the same – they each have different goals, and as such, different needs. Below, we share a few examples of how editing has played out differently in some of the open textbooks that we've supported, so you can see how variable these processes can be.

Perhaps one of the biggest lessons learned to date is around timing and editing. We supported one project in which the project leads decided to keep things moving on a rolling basis, rather than waiting for all the content to be ready before moving it into the editing phase. In this case, a draft editorial workflow was prepared, and as chapter drafts came in from authors (often at different times), the team moved them to the subject matter editor right away, and from there on to peer review. On this project, it was decided that the content editor would also think about structure and take on a more developmental editing role, and that copyediting and proofreading would take place post peer review.

On other projects, we learned about the importance of a developmental edit. The *Media Innovation and Entrepreneurship* open textbook benefitted from the fact that one of the book's lead editors was both a subject-matter expert and experienced editor. A majority of this editor's time on the project was spent conducting a developmental edit of chapters in the book, ensuring the coherency in voice across the book, leading to a more cohesive and valuable resource for students and instructors. With open textbook projects that have multiple authors, this type of edit is extremely useful to check for consistency in structure, tone, voice, and language across the book.

Across multiple projects, we have run into some common questions that seem to recur:

- Should the author, editor, or both makes changes to content?
- What is the clearest way to demonstrate workflow?
- How can timelines be effectively communicated and reinforced?
- How do we share common tools for editing, formatting, and revisions?

Giving your team some clarity over ownership, practices, and deadlines during the editing phase will make the process smoother. (And trust us, we've had to learn the hard way!)

When something does go wrong (and it almost always will), there are some effective techniques for handling difficult situations with care and equanimity:

- Talk face-to-face with those involved, and if you can't be in the same room, at least try to be on-screen with each other.
- Consult frequently with your leadership team, soliciting and listening to their feedback.
- Make sure that the owner of the editing process is the messenger of news (good or bad).

- If you're the editorial process owner, feel confident when asking for changes to a chapter, and feel free to point to signed MOUs if you needed to confirm your rights to use the content.

- As the project manager or lead of the editorial team, you are the ultimate decision makers for your open textbook. If you can't get the content into a state with which you are comfortable, you are not obliged to include it in the release.

NEED FURTHER ASSISTANCE?

We hope these suggestions will help you plan and oversee the various editing phases of your project. We'll continue to add to this guide as we work with more projects, and we welcome your ideas on what else we could add, or your feedback on how these approaches have worked (or not!) for you.

If you have questions, or anything to add, please let us know in the Rebus Community project home.

 *This work is licensed under the Creative Commons Attribution 4.0 International License.*

Hiring Editors

An open textbook needs most of the types of editing described in our Editing Overview. However, depending on the authors' and project leads' expertise, some editorial functions may be combined, expanded, or compressed. For example, a book authored by an English professor might need less copyediting than one by someone in another discipline (or maybe not!). In other cases, the project leads may be able to double as content (subject-matter) editors, by providing input during the project scoping and outline creation stages.

Whether you rely on volunteers from your team or pay professional editors during this phase, the process allows you to incorporate external and/or non-expert feedback, making the book more accessible for all kinds of readers.

Regardless of the project leads' areas of expertise, however, we advise bringing in an outside copyeditor and developmental editor if you have the funding to do so. The developmental editor will help with the structure and presentation of content, and the copyeditor adds professional objectivity and fresh eyes. Content editors and substantive editors are likely more willing to volunteer their time (although we encourage you to pay them too, if possible), so focus your hiring efforts where they are most needed.

If you have the resources to outsource all the editing on your project, remember that you may need to bring in more than one person. Most editors don't provide (or excel at) a full spectrum of editing services, so it's worth being specific when you ask about their experience. We suggest looking at editorial associations such as the Editorial Freelancers

Association (EFA) and the American Copy Editors Society, or freelancing sites such as Upwork. It's also good to ask around in your professional networks, and perhaps ask for referrals for editors who might have worked on similar projects in your field. Note that costs will vary according to the type of work being done, the editor's experience level, and other factors, such as subject matter or technical expertise required. Be prepared for a range of hourly rates, anywhere from $25 to $125 (or more). The EFA has a helpful list of rates for freelancers, so we encourage you to take a look at them while carefully considering your project's editorial needs.

For those looking for the least expensive path, we recommend that the project leads do a first round of subject matter and content editing. After that, they can hand the book off to a developmental editor to look at as a whole, and finally to a versatile copyeditor who is familiar with your style guide.

NEED FURTHER ASSISTANCE?

We hope these suggestions will help you hire external help during the editing phases of your project. We'll continue to add to this guide as we work with more projects, and we welcome your ideas on what else we could add, or your feedback on how these approaches have worked (or not!) for you.

If you have questions, or anything to add, please let us know in the Rebus Community project home.

FEEDBACK & REVIEW

Peer Review Process Summary

The quality, comprehensiveness, clarity, and currency of open textbooks are often called into question because of a lack of understanding about how OER are created. Foregrounding the peer review process is an important way to dispel these notions, while also ensuring the high quality of your text. As a publicly visible indicator, peer review also signals to potential adopters that this content is suitable for classroom use.

This summary covers aspects of managing pre-publication peer review, while noting that post-publication reviews from readers and adopters is invaluable for future versions and editions.

<table>
<tr><td>

Underlying principles

Review allows experts to share their knowledge. Beyond the credibility that they provide, peer reviewers' critical feedback and suggestions tend to improve the resource for its intended audience.

Decide early on what you need from this process. Determine your goals and expectations before you bring on reviewers, so they can focus on giving you exactly what will be most useful.

Be aware of the differences in perception attached to different types of peer review. Although we think all kinds of review are equally valuable and prestigious, others can perceive anonymous review (similar to double-blind review) differently to non-anonymous review. Weigh these differences as you see fit for your project.

</td></tr>
</table>

Model good behaviour. Set an example with how you communicate with reviewers, so that they communicate equally respectfully with authors. Provide pointers on how to give constructive feedback and critique without losing what's working about the book, and without devaluing the work that's gone into it so far.

Who's Involved?

There's a surprising number of people from your team who can take part in the peer review phase:

- Review coordinator: prepare the review guide, write calls for reviewers, manage recruitment, track progress, and relay information among reviewers and the authoring and editing team

- Reviewers: subject-matter experts who provide critical input and suggestions to improve the resource. (We recommend at least two reviewers per book or per chapter, if you are conducting a chapter-based review)

- Authors: incorporate reviewers' feedback, communicate with editors and reviewers (directly or through the review coordinator)

- Editors: coordinate with the authors and reviewers (or review coordinator) about revisions to the book, implement these revisions in some cases

- Project manager: communicate with the review coordinator (or act as one), share calls for reviewers and project updates

Key Tactics

Peer review generally takes place once all the content has been written and edited, but it can also happen on a rolling basis if you are conducting a chapter-based review. In both cases, it's important to do some prep work so that the process runs smoothly from start to finish:

- Prepare a review guide with a simplified version of your project summary, links to the book or content, general reviewer guidelines, project-specific questions you want addressed, deadlines, tools, reviewer etiquette, compensation (if any), and ways in which reviewers will be credited.

- Create a call for reviewers that includes project details, intended audience level, criteria for reviewers, and instructions for indicating interest. The call should also encourage members of underrepresented groups or those in diverse cultural, geographic, or social contexts to participate.

- Share the call widely, in the Rebus Community networks, in your team's social media and professional networks, on listservs, and even through cold calls.

- Write up a peer review workflow, so everyone involved understands what the onboarding process is for reviewers.

- Decide on the review tools you'll use, e.g., Google Docs, Hypothes.is, email memos, etc.

- Keep an updated tracking sheet showing reviewers' progress and when check-ins have been conducted.

- Include a Review Statement in your book, both as a way to signal the quality of the book to potential adopters, and as a way to show appreciation for the reviewers' service.

- Communicate with reviewers both during review and after—including when changes are being incorporated, during release, and as the book is adopted. (Reviewers can become eventual adopters.)

- Credit the work that reviewers have done in your team communications, and if possible, send reviewers a thank you card, personal email, or print copy of the book.

Reviewers are often involved because they believe in the value of the project, and we hope these suggestions will help you make it an enjoyable experience for them, while also receiving the feedback you need for your resource.

Read on to learn more about conducting peer review on your open textbook.

Peer Review Process Guide

This section of *The Rebus Guide to Publishing Open Textbooks (So Far)* will help you coordinate and implement peer review on your book, including advice on deciding what type of review is needed, the tools to use, creating a guide for reviewers, and more. It is licensed under a Creative Commons Attribution 4.0 International License (CC BY) and you are welcome to print this document, make a copy for yourself, or share with others.

Please read through the sections below, and consider the suggestions as you begin the peer review stage of your project. If you have any questions or feedback, please feel free to post them in the Rebus Community project home. This document is an evolving draft, based on our experience managing open textbook projects and community feedback. We welcome your thoughts and contributions, so let us know how it works for you, or if you have any suggestions to improve the guide.

WHAT IS PEER REVIEW AND WHY DOES IT MATTER?

Review is the process in which subject experts read through content and provide critical feedback and suggestions to improve the resource for its intended audience. It can take place at many stages in the publishing process. When we speak about **peer review**, we are typically talking about review that takes place before your book is published or officially released. However, peer review can also take place after the book is released – called **post-publication peer review**. This guide will largely focus on **pre-publication peer review**, which can take place at a few different stages before the book is published.

Peer review is invaluable for ensuring the **quality of educational content**, and is integral to the production of textbooks, just as it is for scholarly monographs and journals. Its presence signals to a prospective adopter that the work has passed through rigorous quality control, and that its content is suitable for use in the classroom.

This is especially significant when working with OER, as the quality, comprehensiveness, clarity, and currency of open textbooks and open educational resources (OER) is often called into question by naysayers. OER, due to their low-cost nature and ease of creation/publication, are mistakenly perceived as **low-quality**. Peer review is important to **dispel these notions**, and to **encourage wider use and adoption** of the book – which is ultimately the goal of most projects. Not only does it give a public indicator of quality to potential adopters, but experience tells us reviewers very often end up adopting the text they've reviewed themselves, so it's great 'advertising.'

External perception aside, peer review is fundamentally a means for you to receive **valuable feedback** on your book's content and make it stronger. It's a chance for you to share your book with subject experts and **ensure that the content is appropriate, accurate, and adequately covers the material**.

GETTING STARTED

If you're reading this guide, chances are you've decided that you want your book to go through peer review. But how do you actually go about organizing this process? The first step should be to decide who is in charge. It may be that you're happy to coordinate the process, but if you need help, or you don't want to have contact with your reviewers, we recommend recruiting a **review coordinator**. Whoever acts as the coordinator, they will be responsible for preparing the review guide, managing recruitment, tracking reviewers' progress, and relaying information between the reviewers and the authors, editors, and/or project managers as needed.

Once you have a coordinator (and have briefed them about your project if they're new to the team) there are a few things that you and your team should discuss. The first is to consider what you would like to get out of the peer review process – are their particular **expectations** or **goals**? For instance, you may want peer reviewers to ensure that the book's content and tone are consistent for an undergraduate audience at the first-year level. Or you may want to assess whether there are any major gaps in the content that need fleshing out, etc. Setting these goals will make it easier to prepare a guide for reviewers, recruit the right experts, and ensure that you get something useful out of this process.

You should also be clear about how important the external perception of the review is to you – some potential adopters might expect formal, double-blind review, whereas others just want to know there have been several sets of eyes on the content along the way. There are good arguments for both sides of this, and only you can know what's right for your project.

Finally, while you have your team together, you should discuss at **what stage** you would like to share the content with reviewers – before it has been edited, or after. One advantage of sharing content with reviewers after it has been edited is that the reviewer can focus more on subject matter, structure, tone, etc. than looking for grammatical errors. On the other hand, conducting review and incorporating feedback after a substantial edit does introduce the possibility of more errors requiring a second round of corrections. This choice might be affected by the resources you have access to as a project. Do note, though, that other project tasks could be taking place while review is ongoing (such as accessibility checks, glossary development, permissions, etc.), so there's no need to bring you project to a halt for this stage.

TYPES OF PEER REVIEW AND TOOLS: WHAT'S RIGHT FOR YOU?

Before you begin looking for reviewers, it's important to decide **what kind of peer review** you would like to conduct on your project. In academic and educational publishing, there are many terms that are used for different types of peer review. At Rebus, we like to keep things simple, so for us, the biggest choice is **whether your review will be anonymous or not**.

In an anonymous peer review process, authors and reviewers' identities will be unknown to one another and, potentially, editors. Conversely, if you don't want to keep the process anonymous, these identities will be known, which might allow authors, editors, and reviewers to be in communication if need be. When deciding which is right for you, look back on the goals that you had set with your team earlier – if your priority is to follow a largely formal/traditional process for the perceived "prestige" value (we think all kinds of review are equally valuable and prestigious, but the reality is that opinions and perceptions differ), you might want to keep things anonymous. Or, if you want to be able to engage collaboratively with and publicly credit volunteers, you may want to know who they are from the start. What's important is that you have experts looking through the book, and identifying areas for improvement.

You should also decide whether you would like reviewers to read through the **full-text** or a **chapter** or another section of the book, such as a **part**. Some combination of these can also be valuable – most often with 1-2 reviewers for each chapter, then another 1-2 for the full text. Full-text reviewers would be able to better comment about the structure of the book, whereas chapter or part-level reviewers would be able to provide more granular comments about those sections. For a full-text review, you will need to wait until all the content has come in, whereas chapter-level review could take place on a rolling basis as content is submitted.

Also consider **how many reviewers** you would like to have for each section, remembering that you can always adjust if you have more or less of a response than you expect. Typically, academic and scholarly works will have a minimum of 2 peer reviewers. However, this number can vary based on your project's discipline, the topics covered in the book, the reviewers' areas of expertise, available formats, audience, intended use (e.g. in classrooms or as a library resource), and whether the reviewer is asked to look at the full-text or a single chapter/section.

Lastly, you should take a look at the different tools available for reviewers to provide feedback. You may want reviewers to look at content in **Google**

Docs, and leave comments or edits using the Suggestion mode. This option might be ideal if you are asking reviewers to look at content that has not been edited yet. Or, you might want reviewers to look at the content and leave feedback using a web annotation tool like **Hypothes.is**. This option would be preferred if your content is already formatted, in Pressbooks, for instance. Alternatively, you could ask reviewers to write a **memo** and share it with the review coordinator via email. We've prepared some templates with instructions for reviewers using either Google Docs or Hypothes.is, which you are welcome to adapt for your review guide.

CREATING A REVIEW GUIDE

Once all the major decisions regarding the review process have been made, you can turn your attention to preparing guidelines for reviewers. This may be something the review coordinator takes on, or might be a **team effort**, with input from the project managers and editors.

If you like, you could start with our review guide templates (one for reviewers using Google Docs or another for those using Hypothes.is), and **fill in information about your project**. Make sure to include details about the **audience**, **guiding questions** specific to the project (these should tie into the goals discussed earlier), **deadlines** (multiple, if review is taking place on a rolling basis), **tools** and how to provide feedback, and **compensation** (if any) or other ways that reviewers will be credited or recognized in the project and final text.

It's important to include a few lines about **reviewer etiquette**, to remind reviewers that they are critiquing the work that someone may have pored hours into writing. Conversely, be sure to thank reviewers for their service! Reviewers are often involved because they believe in the value of the project, especially if they're volunteers, and as the one in charge, you can make sure they enjoy the experience and feel appreciated.

This sample review guide follows the structure outlined above, and includes a separate list of project specific questions that reviewers should keep in mind. However, the structure can be adapted — this example review guide incorporates project specific guiding questions with the core components of review. Both example guides are licensed CC BY, and you can refer to or adapt each as suits your project's needs.

RECRUITING REVIEWERS

Finding peer reviewers can be a challenging task, but far from impossible. We have a separate chapter dedicated solely to recruitment efforts, which you are welcome to read through, but here are some takeaways specific to finding peer reviewers.

The key to successful recruitment is having a **clear and concise call**. Your call should be short, informative, and direct interested candidates to the right place. You should aim to include the following details: a **brief description** of the project, with a link to the public listing page; the **intended audience**; **criteria for reviewers** based on what you'd like to get out of the review process; and clear **directions to volunteer**. Here's a sample call posted on a public forum, and an example of various kinds of copy used for emailing potential volunteers.

You can also include a few lines encouraging members of **underrepresented groups** within the community and people working in **different contexts** to your own to apply (e.g. different regions/countries, different kinds of institutions etc.) – having a wide range of perspectives assessing your content will help to ensure that it meets the needs of all students in the long run!

Before sending out the calls, you should also **be prepared to track responses** from potential reviewers. Use the team's preferred tools, such as Google Sheets, to collect a list of interested candidates, confirmed reviewers, contact information, deadlines, and status. Doing so will make it easier for you to oversee the process, and not have to sift through emails or chats for an update. We're prepared a review tracking template that you could copy and adapt for your project.

Once the call and the tracking sheet are created, you're **ready to send** out your call! A great place to start is **mailing lists or listservs** that are specific to your field or discipline. You can also share the call with the

Rebus Community, on **social media**, and in your **personal networks** (and encourage others on the **team** to do the same). A good option is to have each team member write up a list of all the people they think are qualified and who might be interested, and send them each an email asking them to act as a reviewer. The personal touch goes a long way! It may take a week or two for you to start receiving responses, so be patient, but if you find that you haven't had the response you hoped for, you could also send out **cold calls**. This involves some good old fashioned internet sleuthing to find faculty you think might be suitable for the role. Sending out cold calls is time consuming, and can have low response rates, but if you pick your candidates wisely (making sure their expertise aligns with the project), you might be surprised at how willing people are to be involved.

MANAGING THE REVIEW PROCESS

As responses start filtering in, you can update your tracking spreadsheet and assess whether the respondents are right for the role. Make sure to **respond to reviewers** who have been selected, and offer a note to the ones who haven't! You can **confirm details** with selected reviewers, sharing a copy of the **review guide** and setting a **clear deadline for completion** of the review (we recommend allowing *at least* 4-6 weeks).

During this exchange, you should also (of course) **share the content** with the reviewers, or get this to them as soon as possible. Ideally, you'd like to send content to reviewers immediately after they express their interest in the task, so as to avoid any waiting around.

Once all the details are confirmed and content has been sent, you can let the reviewers start the process and largely leave them be. However, we do recommend a **series of check-ins** leading up to the agreed upon deadline to make sure that the reviewer is all set, that they don't have any questions, and to make sure they are still committed to completing the task. You can check-in as many (or few) times as you like. We recommend doing so:

- 2-3 weeks after you confirm the details with them
- A week before the deadline

- One (business) day after the deadline if they haven't submitted
- Then as often as needed to get a response from them before it is clear they are no longer participating in the project!

The next step is to **collect the reviews** as they roll in, and **pass them along** to authors or editors. Be sure to **send thanks to the reviewers** for their time and feedback. You should encourage them to adopt the book when it is available for classroom use, and let them know you'll share updates about the project with them as things progress.

Depending on the nature of your project and the type of peer review process you have selected, you can also ask reviewers if they would like to communicate with authors or editors as changes are being implemented. And finally, it's also be good to ask reviewers to share their feedback about the process overall, so you can keep it in mind for the rest of the project!

AFTER THE PEER REVIEW

Of course, the 'peer review' stage doesn't end after the review has been submitted, and you've shared your thanks with the reviewers for their work. The obvious next step is to figure out how to incorporate the feedback! This is most often done by the authors themselves, with the editors or project managers coordinating, but sometimes the editors may take on the changes themselves. There are also inevitably decisions around which suggestions to take, and which to defer or leave aside. We'll have some guidance on how to handle this portion of the review in future.

Aside from working on the content, there are a last couple of threads to tie up after the review, but they aren't very intensive, as you'll see.

First of all, we suggest you **send ongoing updates about the project to reviewers**, especially when the book is released. More often than not, they're excited to hear about the progress, and (very importantly!) they could be **potential adopters** once the book is out. Share the announcement of the book's release with them, and encourage them to spread the word in their institutions and networks – as reviewers, they're in the perfect position to vouch for the text.

Once all the reviewers have shared their feedback and changes have been made to the content, it's good to include a **Review Statement** in the book back matter. This is an excellent way to indicate to potential adopters that the book has undergone peer review and is a high quality resource. It's also a great chance to list reviewers (if agreed that they'll be credited) and publicly recognize their work on the project. Here's a review statement template that you can work with, and you can take a look at an example statement from another open textbook.

Finally, it's a nice gesture to **send a physical copy of the book to the reviewer** as thanks, if you're printing copies of the book, and have the capacity to do so. Alternatively, a thank you card or personal email can do the trick – or an offer to return the favour and review their future open textbook!

OTHER THINGS TO CONSIDER

While the major aspects of the peer review process are covered above, there are a few last things that might come up. Many open textbook projects don't have much in the way of funding, and often none at all, so financial **compensation** for reviewers won't always be possible. While we do encourage you to look for sources of funding for peer review, we fully understand that this simply may not be possible in all cases. Reviewers may ask about compensation outright, as it is fairly common to be paid for review of other scholarly works, so make sure you have an answer for them. If no funds are available, you could let them know of any other recognition you could provide them, and to reiterate the importance and potential impact of your project. Money isn't the only motivator, so share a bit more about the project and see whether this inspires them to participate.

At the same time, remember that **reviewers are people too**! They might have their own reasons for not participating, stepping down from the project, or requesting delays. While you have a timeline that you'd like to follow, try to be understanding as the inevitable obstacles or delays come up. Look out for the people involved in your project, and if anyone does have to drop out of the job they signed up for, think about how else you might be able to keep them engaged.

With all this done, you should be ready to move on to the next stage!

NEED FURTHER ASSISTANCE?

We hope these suggestions will help you coordinate and run a peer review process smoothly. We'll continue to add to this guide as we work with more projects, and we welcome your ideas on what else we could add, or your feedback on how these approaches have worked (or not!) for you.

If you have questions, or anything to add, please let us know in the Rebus Community project home.

Review Guide Template (Google Docs)

REBUS COMMUNITY REVIEW GUIDE

Welcome to the guide for Rebus open textbook reviewers. This guide is meant to help you give great, useful feedback on the open textbooks we are helping to develop. You are welcome to print this Google doc, make a copy for yourself, or share with others.

Please read through sections below, and use this as a reference as you complete your review. If you have any questions, email the project lead.

BEFORE WE BEGIN

As we strive to work openly, all contributions made to this textbook will be licensed under a CC BY 4.0 International License. Your name will be mentioned in the published version of the book as reviewer.

No OER textbook can serve all learners, so it is important to be aware of the context the book is meant to live in. Take a moment to read through the project summary to familiarise yourself with the book's purpose and audience before beginning your review.

ABOUT THIS BOOK

Include a quick summary and description of your project and book here. You should also link to project info page, so interested readers can learn more.

AUDIENCE

Insert a few sentences about the book's intended audience here. For example: "This book is meant for use in first-year introductory courses. The audience will primarily consist of undergraduates pursuing the major, however can also include some mixed-major undergraduates." You can include as much detail as you think is necessary, such as technical requirements, reading levels, etc.

CORE COMPONENTS

If there were one single question your review should seek to answer, it should probably be:

"To what extent is the book successful in meeting the needs of its primary market?"

— tonybates.ca

When reviewing drafts, also consider:

1. **Comprehensiveness:** The text covers all areas and ideas of the subject appropriately and provides an effective index and/or glossary.

2. **Content Accuracy:** Content is accurate, error-free and unbiased.

3. **Relevance Longevity:** Content is up-to-date, but not in a way that will quickly make the text obsolete within a short period of time. The text is written and/or arranged in such a way that necessary updates will be relatively easy and straightforward to implement.

4. **Clarity:** The text is written in lucid, accessible prose, and provides adequate context for any jargon/technical terminology used.

5. **Consistency:** The text is internally consistent in terms of terminology and framework.

6. **Organization Structure Flow:** The topics in the text are presented in a logical, clear fashion.

7. **Grammatical Errors:** The text contains no grammatical errors.

8. **Cultural Relevance:** The text is not culturally insensitive or offensive in any way. It should make use of examples that are inclusive of a variety of races, ethnicities, and backgrounds.

This rubric was developed by BCcampus Open Education. This work is licensed under a Creative Commons Attribution 3.0 Unported license.

PROJECT SPECIFIC QUESTIONS

This is where you can add guiding questions for reviewers that are specific to your project. This helps to draw their attention to any areas you think need particular consideration, and helps ensure the feedback you receive is valuable.

LEAVING FEEDBACK

Please leave feedback in the Google doc using either the Comments tool or by providing feedback with the Suggestions tool.

Commenting

Leave a comment in the document by selecting a portion of text, and clicking on the comment icon.

Alternatively, you can select the text, and choose Insert > Comment on the menu at the top of the page, or use the keyboard shortcut for your computer. You can select individual words or whole sentences, leaving feedback on specific parts of the document.

Once you enter your comment, be sure to click on "Comment" to save it. Once it is saved, it will appear next to the selected text. You can edit or delete a comment by clicking on the ellipsis in the top right corner of the comment.

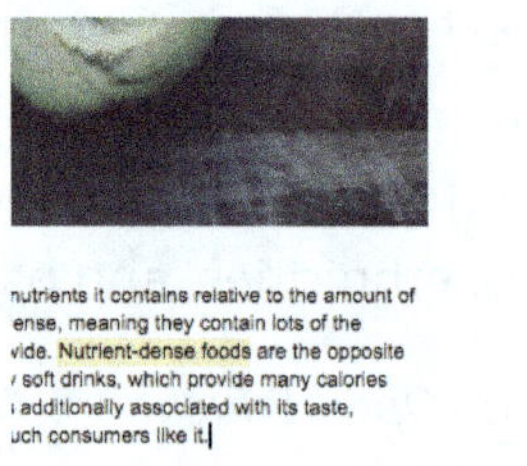

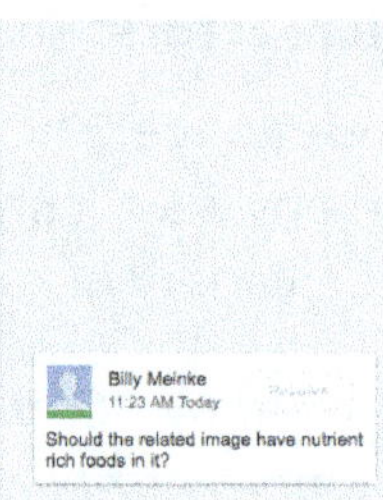

Suggesting

You can also leave proposed edits in the document by switching to Suggesting mode in the upper right-hand part of the document.

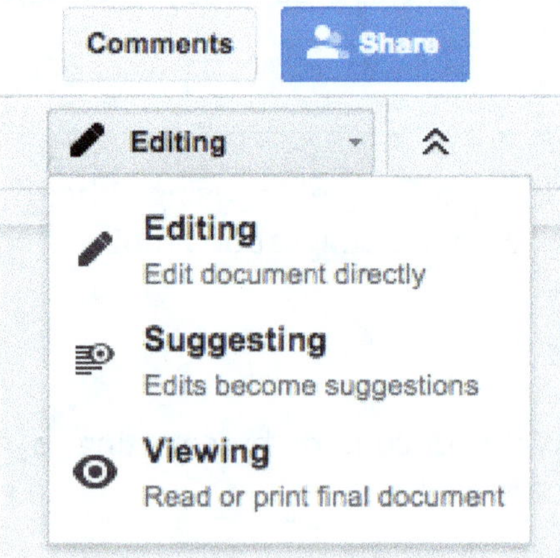

Similar to track changes features of other word processing programs, the authors will see your proposed change and selectively roll or edit them in.

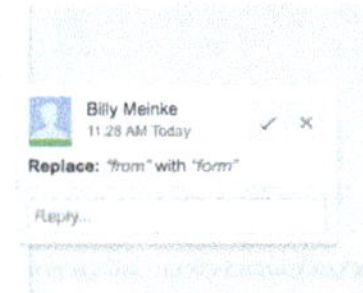

When in doubt, begin by leaving comments. Use the Suggesting mode as it is useful to you.

Reviewer Etiquette

Here you can add a few sentences about reviewer etiquette. The following is a short example, but could be expanded on, particularly if authors will see reviewer comments – you may want to mention this specifically.

When leaving feedback, please be conscious your language and tone and remember that the content you are critiquing is the product of many hours of concerted labour. Keep your criticism constructive, and avoid using derogatory phrases, or making personal remarks about the author. As a courtesy to the author or editor, avoid using abbreviations or short forms of words when providing feedback. Doing so ensures that your feedback remains clear and easy to understand for everyone.

If you run into any issues during this process, please contact the project lead.

DEADLINE

Specify the deadline for completion of review here.

COMPENSATION

If financial compensation is available for reviewers upon completion of the review, you can mention so here.

RECOGNITION FOR REVIEWERS

If you plan to credit reviewers in a review statement, or elsewhere in the book, make a note of it here.

REFERENCES

- http://llt.msu.edu/guidelines/copyeditingguidelines.pdf
- http://www.unm.edu/~ldbeene/Editing.pdf
- http://www.collegeopentextbooks.org/textbook-listings/how-to-be-a-reviewer
- http://www.tonybates.ca/2015/06/24/guidelines-for-reviewing-an-open-textbook/
- http://open.umn.edu/opentextbooks/ReviewRubric.aspx

Find an editable version of this template here.

Review Guide Template (Hypothes.is)

REVIEW GUIDE (HYPOTHES.IS): TEMPLATE

Welcome to the guide for Rebus open textbook reviewers. This guide is meant to help you give great, useful feedback on the open textbooks we are helping to develop. You are welcome to print this Google doc, make a copy for yourself, or share with others.

Please read through sections below, and use this as a reference as you complete your review. If you have any questions, you can email the project lead.

BEFORE WE BEGIN

As we strive to work openly, all contributions made to this textbook will be licensed under a CC BY 4.0 International License. You will be credited as a reviewer in the published version of the book.

No OER textbook can serve all learners, so it is important to be aware of the context the book is meant to live in. Take a moment to read through the project summary to familiarise yourself with the book's purpose and audience before beginning your review.

ABOUT THIS BOOK

Include a quick summary and description of your project and book here. You should also link to project info page, so interested readers can learn more.

AUDIENCE

Insert a few sentences about the book's intended audience here. For example: "This book is meant for use in first-year introductory courses. The audience will primarily consist of undergraduates pursuing the major, however can also include some mixed-major undergraduates." You can include as much detail as you think is necessary, such as technical requirements, reading levels, etc.

CORE COMPONENTS

If there were one single question your review should seek to answer, it should probably be:

"To what extent is the book successful in meeting the needs of its primary market?"

— tonybates.ca

When reviewing drafts, also consider:

1. **Comprehensiveness:** The text covers all areas and ideas of the subject appropriately and provides an effective index and/or glossary.

2. **Content Accuracy:** Content is accurate, error-free and unbiased.

3. **Relevance Longevity:** Content is up-to-date, but not in a way that will quickly make the text obsolete within a short period of time. The text is written and/or arranged in such a way that necessary updates will be relatively easy and straightforward to implement.

4. **Clarity:** The text is written in lucid, accessible prose, and provides adequate context for any jargon/technical terminology used.

5. **Consistency:** The text is internally consistent in terms of terminology and framework.

6. **Organization Structure Flow:** The topics in the text are presented in a logical, clear fashion.

7. **Grammatical Errors:** The text contains no grammatical errors.

8. **Cultural Relevance:** The text is not culturally insensitive or offensive in any way. It should make use of examples that are inclusive of a variety of races, ethnicities, and backgrounds.

This rubric was developed by BCcampus Open Education. This work is licensed under a Creative Commons Attribution 3.0 Unported license.

PROJECT SPECIFIC QUESTIONS

This is where you can add guiding questions for reviewers that are specific to your project. This helps to draw their attention to any areas you think need particular consideration, and helps ensure the feedback you receive is valuable.

LEAVING FEEDBACK

Please leave comments on the web version of the text using Hypothes.is, and/or provide a short memo summarising your feedback. This memo can be submitted to the project lead or review coordinator. Please also notify the lead and coordinator when you have finished making your comments in Hypothesis, if you choose to do so.

How to Use Hypothes.is

In-line Comments

1. Open the chapter you are reviewing in your browser.

2. Open the Hypothesis panel by clicking on the left arrow in the

sidebar.

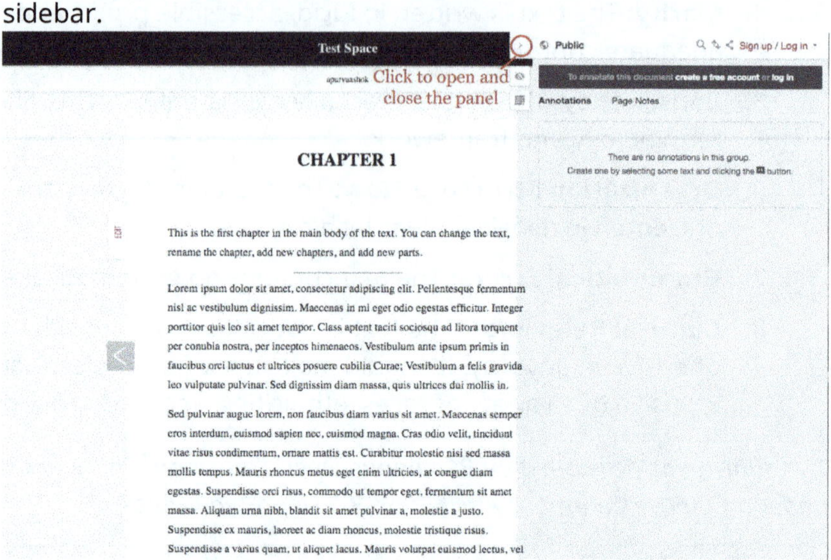

3. Log in using the username and password provided by Rebus (if you have not been provided with these details please contact the project manager).

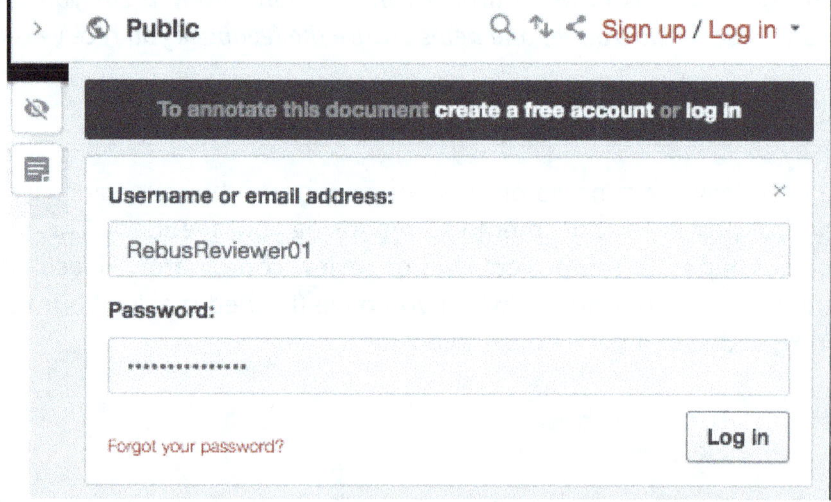

4. By default, Hypothesis annotations are made to the Public group. For the purposes of peer review, a group called Rebus Review has been created. To make annotations to this group, click on the dropdown menu next to **Public**, and select **Rebus Review**. All of

your annotations will now be made in this group, and will remain private.

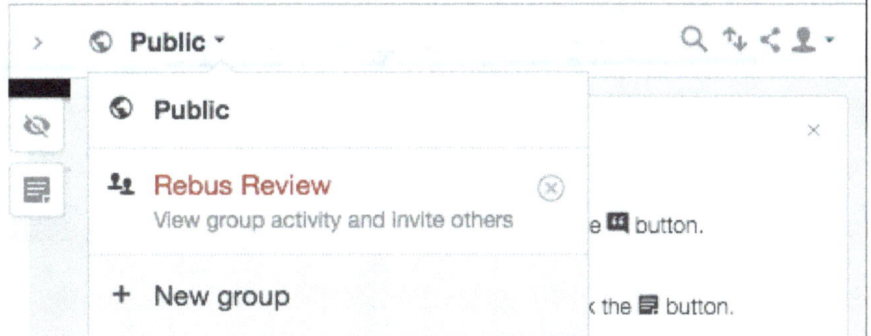

5. Select the text you would like to comment on or highlight.

Lorem ipsum dolor sit amet, consectetur adipiscing elit. Pellentesque fermentum nisl ac vestibulum dignissim. Maecenas in mi eget odio egestas efficitur. Integer porttitor quis leo sit amet tempor. Class aptent taciti sociosqu ad litora torquent per conubia nostra, per inceptos himenaeos. Vestibulum ante ipsum primis in faucibus orci luctus et ultrices posuere cubilia Curae; Vestibulum a felis gravida leo vulputate pulvinar. Sed dignissim diam massa, quis ultrices dui mollis in.

6. Click on Annotate to add a comment. You can type in your comment and click on **"Post to Rebus Review"** to post it in the group.

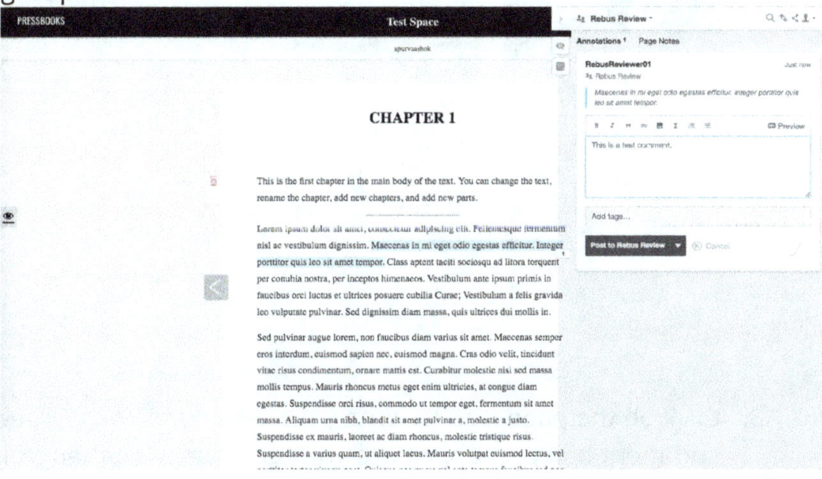

7. You can edit, delete, reply to or share your comment once it has been posted by using the buttons on the bottom-right of the comment box.

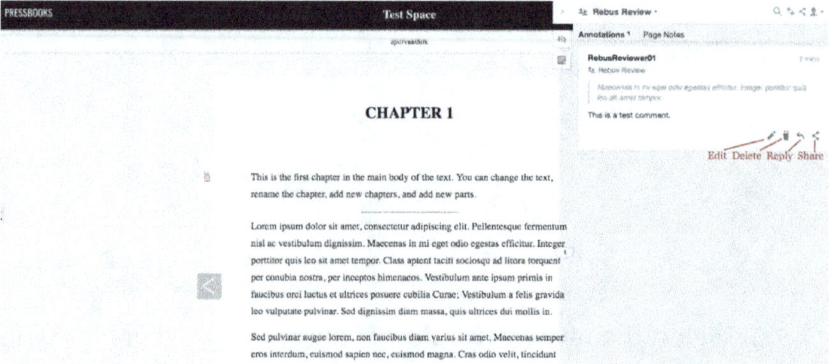

Page Notes

1. Log in to Hypothesis account using the account and password provided by Rebus, as described above, and switch to the Rebus Review group.

2. By default, Hypothesis is set to display and enter annotations. To enter a longer memo-style note, or view other notes on a particular chapter, click on **Page Notes** from the top menu.

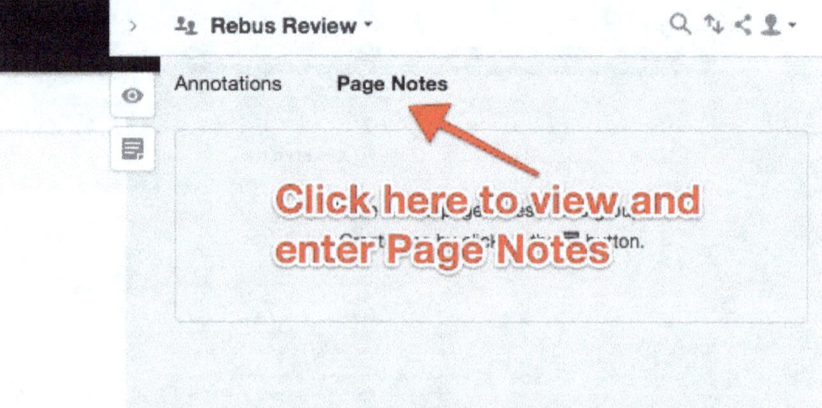

3. Click on the page icon to write your own note. You will see a comment box pop-up, where you can type in your lengthier

comments.

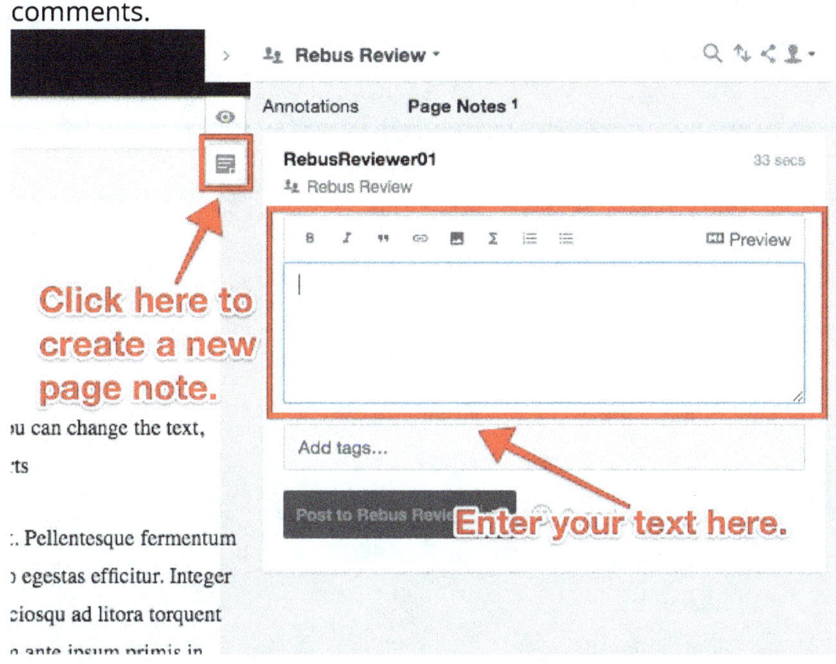

4. Once you have finished typing, click on **Post to Rebus Review** to post your note to the group.

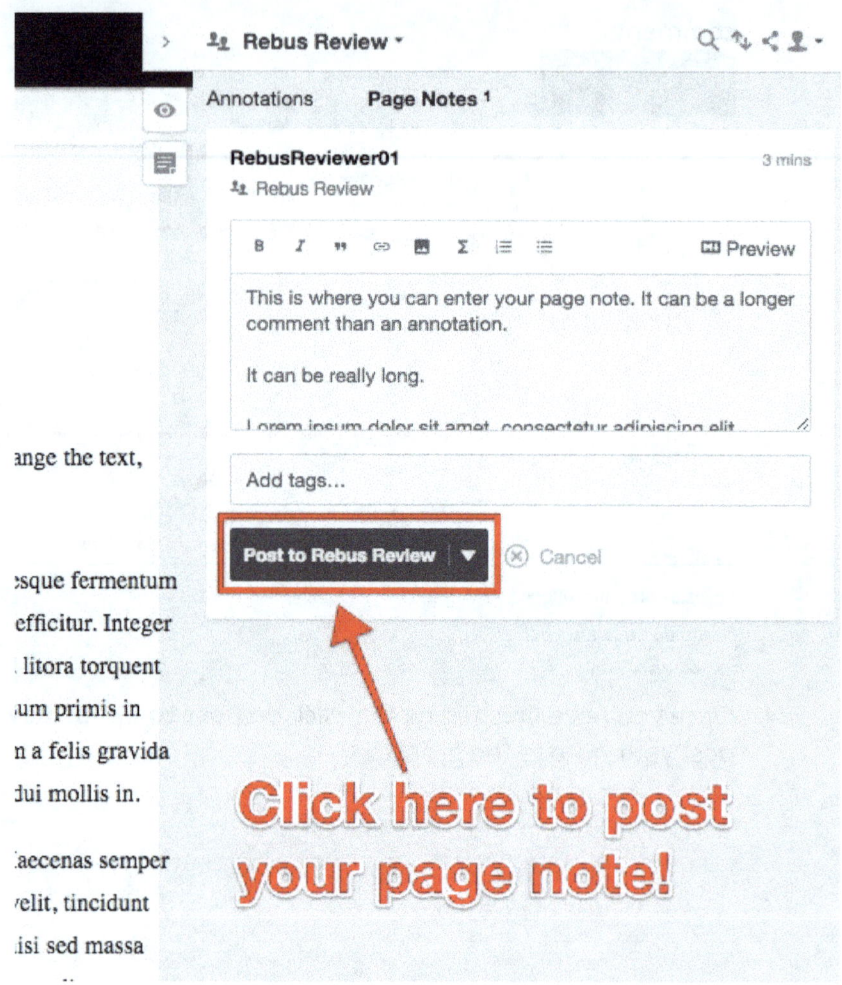

5. You can edit, delete, reply to, or share page notes similar to
   annotations!

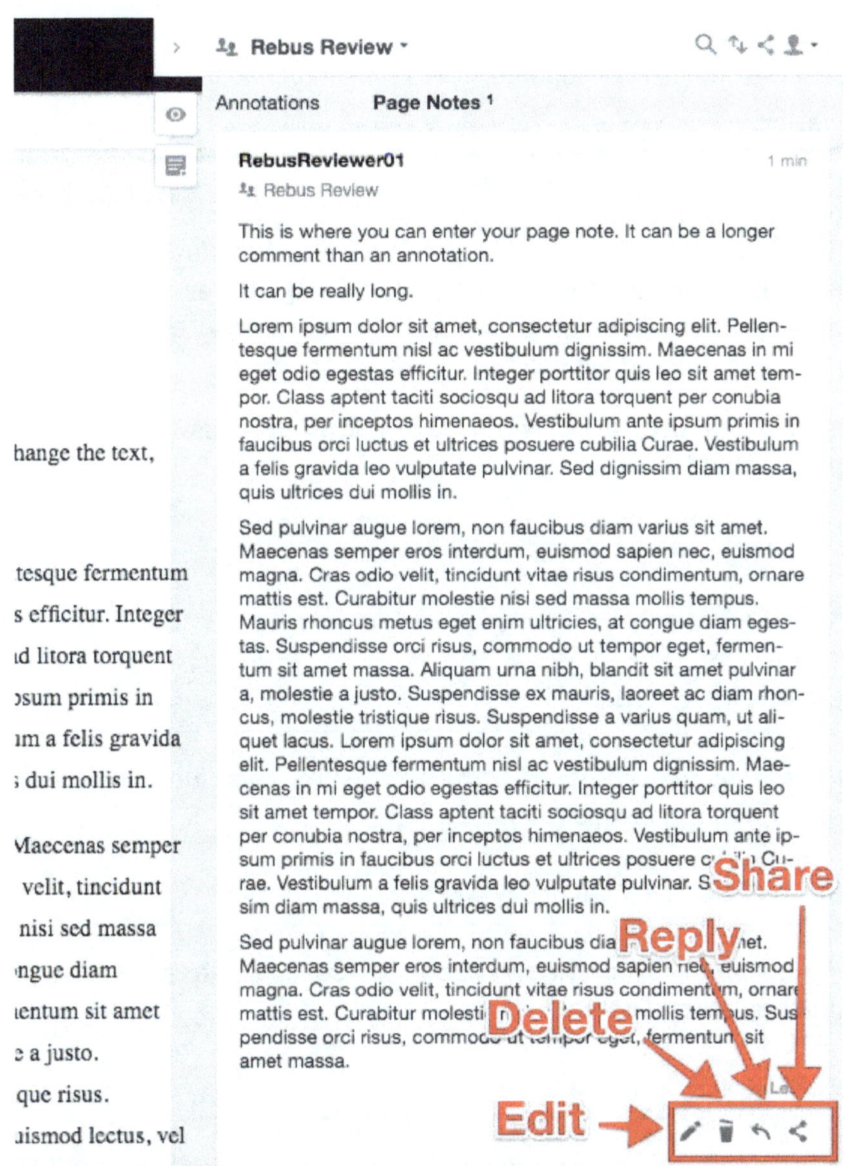

Reviewer Etiquette

Here you can add a few sentences about reviewer etiquette. The following is a short example, but could be expanded on, particularly if authors will see reviewer comments – you may want to mention this specifically.

When leaving feedback, please be conscious your language and tone and remember that the content you are critiquing is the product of many hours of concerted labour. Keep your criticism constructive, and avoid using derogatory phrases, or making personal remarks about the author. As a courtesy to the author or editor, avoid using abbreviations or short forms of words when providing feedback. Doing so ensures that your feedback remains clear and easy to understand for everyone.

If you run into any issues during this process, please contact the project lead.

DEADLINE

Specify the deadline for completion of review here.

COMPENSATION

If financial compensation is available for reviewers upon completion of the review, you can mention so here.

RECOGNITION FOR REVIEWERS

If you plan to credit reviewers in a review statement, or elsewhere in the book, make a note of it here.

REFERENCES

- http://llt.msu.edu/guidelines/copyeditingguidelines.pdf
- http://www.unm.edu/~ldbeene/Editing.pdf
- http://www.collegeopentextbooks.org/textbook-listings/how-to-be-a-reviewer
- http://www.tonybates.ca/2015/06/24/guidelines-for-reviewing-an-

open-textbook/

- http://open.umn.edu/opentextbooks/ReviewRubric.aspx

Find an editable version of this template here.

Review Statement Template

This template may be used as you've concluded peer review on your project. Find an editable version here.

[*Book Title*] was produced with support from the Rebus Community, a non-profit organisation building a new, collaborative model for publishing open textbooks. Critical to the success of this approach is including mechanisms to ensure that open textbooks produced with the Community are high quality, and meet the needs of all students who will one day use them. Rebus books undergo both peer review from faculty subject matter experts and beta testing in classrooms, where student and instructor feedback is collected.

This book has been peer reviewed by [*insert number*] subject experts from [*insert number*] higher education institutions. [*Each chapter/The full-text/ etc.*] received a [*single-blind/double-blind/open*] review from [*one/two/etc.*] reviewer, based on their area of expertise. The reviewers were largely [*academics/professionals/institutional staff*] with required specialist knowledge in [*specify concepts, topics, or fields in your discipline*].

Reviews were structured around considerations of the intended audience of the book, and examined the comprehensiveness, accuracy, and relevance of content. Reviews were also focused on relevance longevity, clarity, consistency, organization structure flow, grammatical errors, and cultural relevance. See the review guide [*please link to the appropriate review guide used for your project*] for more details. Changes suggested by the reviewers covered mainly [*specify areas here*] and were incorporated by [*describe how changes were made*].

[*List names of author(s), project manager(s), review coordinator(s)*] and the team at Rebus would like to thank the review team for the time, care and commitment they contributed to the project. We recognise that peer reviewing is a generous act of service on their part. This book would not be the robust, valuable resource that it is were it not for their feedback and input.

Reviewers included:

- [*list reviewers and affiliated institutions, if review was not anonymous*]

MARKETING & COMMUNICATIONS

Marketing and Communications Summary

When the "product" is an open textbook, "marketing" takes on new meaning. The promotion and communications tools you use may parallel those in conventional marketing, but the underlying principles of openness, collaboration, and inclusion give it them a less sales-driven flavour. In what follows, we share some of the **whys** of 'open marketing', as well as the **hows** of getting it done.

Underlying principles

Marketing starts at day one, or better yet, day zero. Well before content is written, even before a project officially 'starts', the story of the textbook has begun, including the reasons for creating it, the subject it covers, your team approach, and people who make up that team. Get in the mindset of telling that story early and often.

Every open textbook project is different: so is the marketing. Our suggestions are a guideline, not a standard. Formulate your own suggestions, based on what happens in your project, and share them with the larger community in the forum!

Collaboration in marketing is as important as it is in content creation. The more voices and perspectives that are brought in, the greater the diversity, which also leads to greater potential for adoption, use, and re-use.

Connection-making is at the heart of communications. Create and tell a story about your project, connect with those who listen, and respond to their feedback.

Who's Involved?

Marketing and communications can be done by anyone on the team, but not everyone thinks of themselves as a "marketing person." That is why it's best to provide a clear outline of the promotional plan, along with the resources your team members will need to communicate with a consistent message. Some of the roles are:

- Project leaders: who create the plan and decide on the strategies to deploy

- Communications lead: who assembles the promotional material, writes a project summary, composes tweets and other blurbs

- Contributors: who can provide (or solicit) reviewer blurbs, endorsements, and recommendations for communications channels

Key Tactics

Word of mouth and grassroots efforts are easily the most effective tactics for marketing your open textbook. The team working on your textbook is one community, but you and everyone else in it has ties to many other communities and can help the word get out! To that end:

- Share content updates, success stories, and key milestones.

- Use every step as a communications opportunity and keep content flowing outward.

- Showcase the team members behind the work –make it personal!

- Share aspects of inclusivity, accessibility, and diversity in your concept, content, and design.

- Engage with new ideas and opinions to connect with relevant, current discourse.

- Tell your stories honestly and transparently.

- Provide accessible feedback tools, so that communication can be two-way.

- Repetition is good: get the word out early and often, using different channels:

  - blog posts

  - social media (with links to useful content)

  - listservs (in your discipline and across communities)

  - email signatures

  - conferences

  - webinars

Like all the processes in publishing openly, marketing and communications may happen in non-chronological order, and/or in unexpected ways. Make everyone on the team a part of it, and nurture their involvement as ambassadors for the book. If you all think about marketing as **producing value in the world by sharing your resource's content**, this will allow it to find its market – those readers, adopters, and adapters who need it.

Read on to explore the whens and hows of marketing and communicating your open textbook project.

Marketing & Communications Overview

This part of *The Rebus Guide to Publishing Open Textbooks (So Far)* is designed to help you think through the process of getting your textbook in front of the people who want it, whether for adoption or adaptation, reading or research. It is about using the tools and strategies of marketing and communications to reach those users, but also about the ways in which publicity, promotion, messaging, and outreach tend to differ when the "product" is an open textbook. Like everything related to publishing open textbooks, these processes often happen on variable schedules, and collaboration is always key to make them successful. In many ways, the marketing and communications of Rebus-supported projects start right at the conception of the work, running through to release as well as far beyond!

In what follows, we take you through what you need to know when telling your project's story and helping it find its audiences. Read through the sections below, and consider our perspectives as suggestions that you can adapt to suit your own unique needs. As you start scoping out your project, and at every other phase along the way, keep marketing and communications in mind. If they run in parallel to the writing, editing, and production phases of creating your resource, everything should go more smoothly when it comes to the big release.

Remember that this part of the *Guide*, like the others, is a summary of what we have learned in working with you. What makes your open textbook project unique, however, also makes it distinctive when it comes to marketing. That means that queries will arise and clarifications will be needed, and we eagerly welcome them! Post your responses to this material in the Rebus Community project home, including questions and concerns that have come up for you. This document will continue to evolve, based on our experience managing open textbook projects and your feedback.

Special thanks to Elizabeth Mays, (former) marketing manager for Rebus; current director of sales and marketing for Pressbooks and adjunct faculty at Arizona State University; and author and editor of two open textbooks (*Media Innovation and Entrepreneurship* and *A Guide to Making Open Textbooks With Students*) for contributing to this overview!

THE REBUS MARKETING PHILOSOPHY

Before diving into tips and suggestions for handling marketing and communications on your open textbook project, we want to explain our philosophy and approach. Rebus' version of marketing differs from the structured, sales-oriented processes that most people might think of. It's not about driving consumer behaviour, leveraging certain needs, notifying prospective customers about product rebates, or increasing purchase rates. Our approach is to **start certain processes right at the beginning of the work**, always with the goal of reaching potential adopters. Starting this early means you have a head start once your book is released, so marketing should be as much a part of the creation process as project scoping and building your team. If you limit your marketing and communications efforts to the time immediately surrounding the release and launch, you may not be as successful in gathering the widest group of readers and adopters around your textbook.

We subscribe to the idea that **marketing is a series of connections**. In most cases, these connections are between *people* and *projects*, where Rebus' target audiences are *collaborators* and *communities*. We see marketing as a way of **creating and telling a story** about your project and the resource you (and others) are working to build. Then, by **forming connections** with those who listen and respond to this story, you can help people find the textbook and help the textbook find its people.

THE PRINCIPLES UNDERLYING OUR APPROACH

Our goal with open textbook projects has always been to create a valuable resource for others to use, and to build a vibrant community around it. Over time, we have landed on a set of principles that are at the core of our overall approach, shared below.

For us, **marketing starts at day one, or better yet, day zero**. Even before the content is scoped out and written, the story of that textbook has begun. The story includes not only the reasons for creating the resource, but also the people who you hope will read, adopt, and adapt it. That means thinking about how your team is formed, who those people are, and what they bring to the project. Simultaneously, as you scope out the chapters and sections and subsections, bring in the story of what the book will include – and what it won't (and why). Keep the communications flowing. Document your decisions and share them with the team, so that they become not just part of the story, but the storytellers themselves. **Get the word out early and often**, about what you're doing and why, as well as who is helping you do it. It can be through word of mouth, social media, association listservs, a blog site, or other channels (we'll dive in to this in more detail later).

Every stage of the open textbook publishing process can be leveraged to help the book reach its potential adopters, and there are ways to ensure that **marketing is smoothly built in to what you do**. For instance, collaborative authorship creates opportunities for buy-in and allows for a native network of ambassadors for the book to form. Project updates (through the channels noted above) keep the creation process on the radar of your colleagues and community, including those who aren't directly involved or interested (yet!) The beta-testing and peer-review phases not only provide invaluable feedback on the book's content, they also help establish groups of future users and readers around the book. Think of these people as **a community of interest and practice,** that naturally forms (and belongs) around the book. In fact, an underlying goal for every stage of open textbook development should be community building and engagement. As long as you are **open about your processes** and communicate them directly, you can always **consider marketing as part of any phase of publishing**.

In our experience so far, providing "value" to a community of potential users or collaborators is one way to help make a book meaningful and visible to them. For instance, one easy way to create value is to turn parts of the textbook's story into useable, engaging, and even teachable chunks. You could do this by **providing content updates** as your team members write and edit their chapters. You can also **share success stories** of things that go well in the process, which not only communicates how open publishing works, but also gives others the incentive to try it out themselves.

When sharing your stories, try to **showcase the team members** behind the work. People like to hear about the personal aspects of publishing, not just the facts and figures. Putting a human face or voice to the project helps make it more compelling, and more relatable for those who aren't involved. Besides, the people who are mentioned will naturally help promote those stories themselves! One way to showcase individual voices is by soliciting and sharing quotes from the team. Ask people both from within and outside the project leadership to talk about their experiences. Beyond the insights you gather on what works (or doesn't) about a given chapter or section, it keeps the process open and adds energy to the community around the book. At the end of the day, the project is made up of you and the team involved, so don't hide behind the scenes!

Another approach to telling the story of your project is to share how your handling or presentation of a particular subject or topic **makes your book unique.** This might be in the tone of the text, the pedagogical approach, what areas you choose to cover (or not cover!), etc. Another great way in which your text might be unique is that it demonstrates **greater inclusivity** and a wider variety of perspectives and participation, both in the content itself and the teams creating the content. One of the most important principles of publishing openly is that it creates opportunities for more inclusive approaches to content creation, so if you commit to and enact these principles in your project, be clear about the choices you're making and why you're making them. Keep up the messaging about your work as related to accessibility, diversity, and equity, from the project scoping phase through content creation, peer review, and release.

As your project rolls along and you reach different milestones, keep asking yourself whether you've remembered to spread the word lately. With marketing and communications, it's important to **maintain momentum as you are building interest**. While your major goal is to complete your book, resource, or ancillary material, the people around you might be focused on other things. So even as you work to build up community around the project, they need to **keep being engaged with new ideas, updates, and stories**. **Be honest and visible**, upfront about your decisions, and attentive to the comments and suggestions you receive in response.

Finally, marketing and communications are **just as much about listening as they are about broadcasting**. Make sure to give your community **accessible pathways to get back to you** and stay on top of those communications channels. Respond quickly and enthusiastically, and it will reinforce that you are listening and care about what they have to say. If you note any eagerness that seems to go beyond standard interest, you might have a potential team member on your hands! Give them individualized attention and the chance to learn more about your project or participate in it. Especially once there is **more than the initial team** talking about the project, make sure that there are places to engage people in conversation and then give them opportunities to do more than just talk (see our engagement guide for more ideas). **Provide avenues to participate** and, as always, be inviting and welcoming!

WHAT TYPES OF TACTICS CAN YOU EMPLOY?

When you begin thinking about marketing and communications within this framework, there's no limit to the types of tactics you can employ. Below is a short list of ways to promote your project, all along the road to release. Some of these are likely familiar, and some might be new, but either way, think about how they can be undertaken within a philosophy of openness and collaboration. Remember to keep providing value, so that these processes always offer a way for someone to get involved and do more. If people have something they can *use* (e.g.: investigate further, teach about, tweet), it will resonate with them more deeply, and inspire them to become part of the process.

- blog posts (with clear links to more content that is useful to your audience)
- milestone announcements (providing information on what someone can do next, like contribute, review, or adopt)
- social media (either from your accounts or a dedicated project account, sharing updates and other relevant content)
- discoverability (so readers, adopters, and adapters can get their hands on the textbook when they want it), meaning:
    - maintaining a public listing for project
    - submitting completed content to repositories
    - ensuring metadata is comprehensive and accurate
- listserv discussions (so you can become an engaged participant in a community, naturally directing people to your resource)
- email signatures (which can keep the project front of mind as you interact with people)
- community calls (to share updates, gather feedback, and reinforce community building)
- conferences (as opportunities to present, be challenged, make connections, and reconsider what you think you "know" about your project and how to make it better in a future release)
- promotional materials (that not only reinforce the value that your resource brings, but do so in quick and friendly formats), including:
    - slide decks
    - blurbs or review quotes
    - pamphlets
- print copies of the book, for potential adopters (to put a physical presence on their desk – front of view, front of mind!)

- project mailing list (for more frequent and detailed updates, and from which you also allow people to opt-out!)

As we've indicated above, each of the tactics might help to serve a specific goal on your project, such as helping give your book a physical presence, or providing more information on how contributors can get involved in the project. Later in this section, we'll go into more detail about these strategies, including how you can leverage them, what content to send out, which channels to use, and more. Stay tuned!

ULTIMATELY, IT'S ALL ABOUT THE PEOPLE

As we've said earlier, for us, marketing and communication are mainly ways to connect communities and collaborators with your book. At Rebus, what drives our work is the idea that we're **building books to build communities, and building communities to build books**. We strongly believe in the power of groups of people to come together around a particular project, and doing so in ways that help everybody benefit.

It's with this goal in mind that we've outlined the principles and strategies above, and we want to remind you to keep tapping into your biggest resource as you go about marketing your book – **you and your team's network of contacts**! Reach out to these people, whether they are in your professional or personal circles, and remember to listen to their insights about your book.

Positive recommendations about the book from people in the community around it are the most valuable pieces of communications you can 'create.' **Word of mouth** is immensely powerful in the OER space, so be sure to leverage any endorsements about your book – even traditional publishers will tell you that there's no paid tactic that has the same impact as someone vouching for the quality of your resource. This type of handselling can only happen if you engage with the community right from the very beginning of your project, so that they are as invested in the resource as you are, even if they were not directly involved in the production. **Collaborate and create**, and you'll see the community grow along the way. For us, that's what open textbook publishing is all about!

NEED FURTHER ASSISTANCE?

We hope these suggestions will help you market and communicate your project, all throughout its various phases and incarnations. We'll continue to add to this section of the *Guide* as we work with more projects. So whether or not we ask you directly, we always welcome your ideas on what else we could added, based on your first-hand experiences and the stories you've heard in passing. We're also very interested to know your feedback about how these approaches have worked (or not!) for you.

Keep coming back to the Rebus Community project home and help the community learn and grow!

This work is licensed under the Creative Commons Attribution 4.0 International License.

PREPARING FOR RELEASE

Release Summary

The "Big Release" is one of the most gratifying phases of the OER creation process. To make the most of it, a coordinated effort allows the word to get out and the resource to get into people's hands. However large your audience, it's important to take your time with these final steps, to make sure the book is in the best possible shape for release.

<table>
<tr><td align="center">Underlying principles</td></tr>
</table>

Estimate targets, but stay flexible. Plan to have your book released one to three months before the academic term in which you'd like to use it. Set a date during the scoping or content creation phase, but remember to revisit and adjust your timeline if and when things change.

Revisit your initial goals and measures of success. Make sure that the resource meets the objectives you set out early on, in terms of both content and formats.

Preparation and planning makes everything easier. Working to build a community of potential adopters and meet accessibility standards at every stage of the process means you will not be rushing to do so during the final weeks before release.

Have fun along the way. Release isn't all checklists and spreadsheets—it also includes elements like designing an attractive cover, writing stories about your experience making the book, and highlighting the impact the book can have, all with a great group of collaborators!

Savour the moment. Build in time for you and your team to celebrate the moment, and pat yourselves on the back for this incredible achievement. Creating an open textbook is no easy feat, but you've done it!

Who's Involved?

Almost everyone on the team will have a part to play leading up to the book's release:

- Project manager: keeps everything on schedule, coordinates with the team, conducts final checks on the book, creates adoption forms and tracking sheets, notifies the community about the release

- Formatter: converts content into accessible formats for readers (minimum: web, editable, and offline formats), does content layout and styling, adds front and back matter

- Designer: creates an engaging ebook and print cover (which may also be openly licensed), makes other marketing collateral as needed (e.g., pamphlets, slide decks, videos)

- Accessibility reviewer: reviews the formatted book to ensure that formats meet accessibility standards, meets with instructional designers to make sure the book meets all learners' needs (including those with recognized disabilities)

- Proofreader: final check after formatting, to catch any small errors

- Marketing team: updates the book description, prepares a release announcement, collects blurbs about the book to feature on the cover or in communications, creates promotion plan

- Others: help with final checks, submit the book to repositories, set up print on demand, and spread the word

Key Tactics

Once content is finalized, you can start working on some of these processes:

- Work backwards from your target release date to distribute workload and allocate time for tasks.

- Remember technical openness—make your book available in web, editable, and offline formats.

- Also make a print-on-demand format available for those students and teachers who need or prefer a physical format.

- Create a cover that attracts potential adopters, distinguishes your book from others, and shows its personality upfront.

- Include front and back matter that complements the main content, rounds out the appearance of the book, and lends some professionally created appeal.

- Create an adoption form and encourage users to self-report adoptions, and use this information to prove the book's impact.

- Follow accessibility checklists provided by your university or regional boards and prepare an accessibility assessment that shows your book meets these standards.

- Update the book's metadata, check the license, and verify the information on the book's homepage (including links to the Adoption Form).

- Submit the book to institutional and OER repositories or referitories.

- Send copies to the team if possible, or at a minimum, include them in the book's acknowledgements.

- Execute your promotional plan and shout it from the rooftops, and ask the team to do the same!

Release is just one of the many débuts that your book will have. After you send it into the world, it will be used, expanded, and adapted in many other ways. So this phase of the process is about having confidence that the resource is ready to be shared, while also being ready for it to be taken on (and maybe released anew) by the communities of practice that form around it. Then, as it becomes part of the disciplinary landscape, start thinking about a long-term vision, including ancillaries, new versions, and/ or remixes.

Keep reading to find out more about planning and implementing the Big Release.

Release Overview

After the work of scoping, creating, editing, and review is done, it is finally time to share your textbook with the world! This section of *The Rebus Guide to Publishing Open Textbooks (So Far)* takes a deep dive into one of the most gratifying phases of the publishing process: The Big Release (as well as the many small steps that lead up to it). Making your open textbook (or other resources) public requires a coordinated effort, much like the rest of the publishing process. In what follows, we summarize the final tasks that link the creation phases of publishing with those in which you get the word out and the resource into people's hands. We cover formatting and layout, cover design, final proofs, print-on-demand, and more.

As in the other sections of this *Guide*, these suggestions are based on our experience with open textbook projects. If you have questions about this overview, or suggestions for what else we could include, please share them in the Rebus Community project home. This document is an evolving draft, based on what we have learned so far in managing open textbook projects and gathering community feedback. We welcome your thoughts and contributions, including ways to improve the *Guide* overall.

IT STARTS WITH A LITTLE MATH

Timing is important when it comes to release. If you want your textbook to be adopted for a course in a given academic year, for example, then it may need to be released as much as three months in advance of that course start date. (Check with your local institution on their policies regarding textbook adoption deadlines, and assume that anyone wanting to adopt your book will need at least a month to review it and make a decision.)

Alternatively, you might work to the deadline for a course you teach yourself, and be prepared for wider adoptions to happen in the following semester. Instead of thinking in terms of the school calendar, you might want to time the release with another big event, such as a major conference in your field. Or, depending on the type of resource you are creating, you might not need to work towards having it ready for a particular course or time of year at all, and can see how things develop as you go.

In any case, there are two ways to approach working out your release date. One is to figure out an approximate release date right at the very start of your project (e.g., a June release for September adoptions), and the other is to work it out once you're getting close to having all your content written, edited, and reviewed. In fact, don't be surprised if you end up doing both of these! Having a **target release date from the outset can be very useful for keeping things on track and focused**, but realistically, **things can change over time**.

In the first scenario, during the project scoping phase, you can get out your calendar and calculator, and start adding up the number of weeks you estimate the entire process will take. Then, count backwards from your desired release date and see if it's looking realistic. In the second, you can plot out how much work is left to do, and see what release date that gives you, and whether you want to adjust at all to bring it closer, or push it out.

Even if you aren't constrained by a specific target, we still recommend working backwards from a projected release date. In that way, you can see when the preceding phases need to take place, and allow time for processes that are less under your time-management control, like peer review and review by potential adopters.

Regardless of the approach, however, it's important to keep revisiting and re-confirming whether your timelines are on track for release. If you do need to do some schedule rejigging as you go, don't worry—that's normal. There will always be some adjusting on every project. Just remember to chat with your team about where to reduce time spent (and where not to), so the book still comes out when you want. And if it comes down to it, and you need to delay publication, that's okay! What's important is that you and your team are happy with the final resource, and proud of what you decide to share with the world. Besides, as an open resource, either you or your readers and adopters may choose to keep revising it, so "release" is just one of many possible débuts that the book will have.

PREPPING FOR RELEASE

Once your content has been finalized, and closer to your release date, you can start working on some of the processes outlined below. (Some of them, like cover design and front/back matter, can be initiated sooner, but others like formatting and arranging for print-on-demand obviously require the content to be finalized.) We've included a variety of steps that most Rebus-supported open textbooks have gone through prior to release, but you might have ideas for additional steps or, alternately, discover that your project requires fewer.

Formatting

Formatting is the process of converting your content from a word processing file into the format that will be consumed by readers. In the case of OER, content should be made available in a wide variety of formats, including web, offline, and editable formats. While Creative Commons licenses *permit* a range of uses, actual *technical* openness is vital to ensure that those uses are in fact possible (e.g., consider the difference between an openly licensed text available solely as a PDF versus one available in PDF, on the web, and in a downloadable, editable format).

Regardless of the book formatting software that you are using, it's important that you create, at a minimum, one web-based format, one offline, and one editable format of your open textbook. There are many ways in which you can meet this standard, but one of the easiest and most popular in the OER world is to use Pressbooks, an open-source book production software. (In the interest of transparency: We love Pressbooks for how functional and useful it is, and we are a paying client of the software. Moreover, we also share an office with them, as well as a co-founder!) With Pressbooks, you are able to produce professional, platform-agnostic outputs of books in multiple formats. These include: web, PDF (print and digital), EPUB, MOBI, ODT, XML, WXR, and XHTML. You may have access to Pressbooks through your institution, or you can create a one-off book at Pressbooks.com. Rebus also offers access to the Rebus Press for many of our projects that do not have access elsewhere. Let us know if you're in that group.

Formatting also includes styling your text, images, tables, and any other parts of your content. Overall it is about structuring and presenting your content so that it can be used and understood by readers in the best possible way. To ensure consistency throughout the book, we recommend making an inventory of the different types of content you want to have (i.e., learning objectives, case studies, summaries, key takeaways, or other recurring sections in each unit). With that in hand, you can create a "style guide" for each of these categories or elements in the inventory. Then create a template for each, which you can easily apply to every instance of them throughout your book. Not only will this help you create an overall look and feel that is coherent throughout the book, you will also be able to ensure that all types of content are styled and structured the same way. That is, your tables, charts, bullet lists, subtitles, end-of-section questions, etc. will look the same from chapter to chapter, making it easier for your readers to recognize what type of content you are presenting.

During this stage, it is a good idea to talk with the instructional designers and accessibility practitioners on your campus, or in your network, and ensure that the resource meets its learning objectives and is formatted with all readers in mind. Formatting for accessibility is critical. This means, among other things, ensuring that headings are styled for contrast, size, hierarchy, etc., so as to make them both legible and comprehensible for all readers. Similarly, images need to contain alt text, which acts as a machine-readable placeholder when the image itself cannot be viewed. These are small points, but important to think about during formatting, so as to reduce any remediative work that might need to happen after your book is released. For more information about accessibility best practices when creating your open textbook, we highly recommend the *BCcampus Open Education Accessibility Toolkit*.

Cover Design

Some people may think that open textbooks don't require book covers, because they are simply 'digital texts.' In fact, covers are an important way to give your book a face and visually engage potential readers and adopters! What's more, open textbooks can be printed, just like any other book, and it's nice to offer more than just plain text on a plain background.

Book covers also help to attract potential adopters by conveying the book's subject matter and overarching themes. For students and readers who will interact with the book, the cover distinguishes it from other resources, and allows it to show its 'personality' up front. While the possibilities are endless, we suggest keeping book covers simple, and dedicating a reasonable but not excessive time to creating the design. Enlisting the help of a student designer or another volunteer who is looking to grow their portfolio can be a good approach, but make sure to give them a clear briefing on what is wanted, as well as a specific timeline and set of deliverables.

As well, put a clear feedback and decision-making process in place, so that the cover doesn't end up getting stuck in 'design-by-committee' delays. When it comes to visual and textual elements, you may want to use open-source fonts and open-license photographs, so that your book cover can also be openly licensed. Public domain image repositories, and open license platforms such as Unsplash can be great resources. Let us know in the Rebus Community project home about your own go-to image and graphic sources – we'd love to share them!

Front and back matter

Adding front and back matter to your book is a good way to include information that complements or supports the main content, without necessarily being central. It can also help round out the appearance of your book and lend it some of that professionally created appeal. The table below contains a list of common front matter and back matter elements that you can choose to include in your book. (We'll be expanding on these in a later section, so stay tuned!)

Front matter	Back matter
Abstract	About the Team
Acknowledgements	About the Publisher
Copyright Page	Accessibility Assessment
Dedication	Afterword
Epigraph	Appendix
Foreword	Author's / Editor's Note
Image Credits	Bibliography
Introduction	Conclusion
List of Abbreviations	Epilogue
List of Illustrations	Errata
List of Tables	Glossary
Other Books by the Author(s) / In this Series	Index
Praise for this Book	Licensing and Remixing Information
Preface	Review Statement
Prologue	Suggested Reading
Recommended Citation	Versioning History

Adoption & Adaptation

One of the challenges of OER creation is tracking the resource's use following release. In conventional publishing, purchase serve as tracking metrics, but that is not the case with open textbooks. Nonetheless, it's important to know who might be using your resource, and for what purposes, not only to grow the community around your book, but also to provide statistics, calculate savings, and report back to your administration or granting agency, if required. Given the technical challenges of tracking use, we advise you to solicit users to self-report. Learning how your resource is used, and the impact it has on student success and retention, may also help you secure funds to improve the resource, create ancillaries, or work on another OER project.

An easy way to get notifications of new adopters and adapters is to have them fill out an adoption form. (You can take a look at our Adoption Form as an example.) Our form asks for the adopter/adapter's name, institution, course information, current course materials in use, cost, and number of students. Forms can be more detailed if you require additional information. Make sure that you link clearly to the form from your book, from the project's public listing page, and from the release announcement or other communications. The wider the form's reach, the higher the response rate!

Accessibility Assessment

With open publishing, creators are able to take enough time to ensure their resource is accessible and usable by all students and readers from the moment of release. This means planning for accessibility and inclusive design from the very beginning, and executing that plan during the subsequent phases. Then, prior to release, a final check of the resource, across the various formats you produce, ensures that the original goals have been met. We recommend running through an accessibility checklist to determine how your book holds up to these standards. We find this checklist from BCcampus to be a helpful starting point, but you can also use checklists or standards provided by your institution, state, or national governing body.

Once you've completed this work, it's important to then include the assessment in the back matter of your book, so that potential users can determine the suitability of the book for all students. There's also value in surfacing this kind of information for those who may not think of it otherwise, so be transparent and forthcoming with the work you've put in, as well as with any known shortfalls.

Final Checks

Other final checks include a visual test, during which you look at the layout in each format – web, PDF, and ebook – confirming consistency and coherence from beginning to end. (Note that this is not as close a read as you would do during proofreading, but instead, it is a more macro-level verification of the layout.) When you're checking content that is web-native, it's good to confirm that external links are all working, that the information about the book on its landing page is clear and descriptive, and that there is a link your adoption form. Licenses should also be clearly displayed, and contact information can be made available, using email links. Check also that the metadata attached to your book is updated, accurate, and comprehensive – this makes it much easier for your book to be discovered in repositories!

At this point, you may want to have your book proofread (or proofread a second time if you have already done one pass). Someone with fresh eyes can catch little errors that might have been introduced during formatting, or new (minor) edits that you make to the content as you go through all these last checks. Remember, however, that when you're so close to a resource, it may never seem perfect to you, so draw a line (and set a time limit) when it comes to ongoing tweaks and adjustments. Or, if you prefer, start up plans for a second edition, and feed this work into the next project!

Submit your book to repositories

To encourage adoptions or adaptations of your open textbook, it's crucial that you make your book easy to find in various institutional and OER repositories. By submitting your book in multiple repositories, it increases the chances that your book will be discovered by educators and researchers looking for openly licensed content in your field. We recommend submitting to major OER repositories/referotories such as MERLOT, Open Textbook library, BCcampus Library, and OER Commons, in addition to your institutional repository, or other local or national repositories in your region.

Print-on-demand (POD)

Even if your open textbook has been born web-native, there's something to be said about the power of print. Print remains an important option for students, many of whom still prefer to engage with content in a physical format. There are also readers who will opt for print, given that digital and online versions necessitate reliable access to digital devices and an internet connection. Print-on-demand is therefore a good way to support accessibility and choice for students, even if you yourself don't plan to use a print book in teaching.

Giving your book a physical presence can also be invaluable for how your resource is perceived. Some adopters will still prefer to see a printed copy of a book: that materiality can make it all-the-more "real" in their perception.

If you're using Pressbooks, you can easily export a print PDF file that is optimized for printing. If you're using other formatting tools, you should check the specifications and requirements by the print-on-demand service that you plan to use. Some common providers are Lulu, IngramSpark, CreateSpace, and Kindle Direct Publishing.You may also want to look into the printing options at your campus bookstore, or with local printers in your area, as their rates might be more favourable. As this section of the *Guide* develops, we'll be outlining how to set up POD in detail, so check back soon!

Update & involve your community

Be sure to send a notification to your community regarding the release, and if possible, send a token of appreciation to anyone who has had a particularly significant role in the development. This could be as simple as a handwritten thank you card, and/or a print copy of the resource. Many people helped create it, after all, and it's generally a small cost in exchange for a lot of goodwill (and another potential adopter!).

In your book's acknowledgements, it's also a nice gesture of gratitude to include a list of all the team members involved in the project, and those who have been part of its broader community. Sharing your thanks with them publicly makes it clear to everyone who uses the book how important the team has been in shaping it!

If you've been sharing updates about how your project is going, there will likely also be a certain amount of anticipation and enthusiasm about the impending release, which you can tap into in a number of ways. For instance, as you're letting people know that the book is close to release, take the chance to ask people to share some feedback (a short review, a statement of endorsement, etc.) on the book and/or process. You can use their words in your promotional assets, and follows any recommendations they have about where to share the book (e.g., listservs you might not know about).

Promotional Assets

With all the care and thought that has gone into creating the resource, it's only fitting to have a coordinated effort to make as much noise about the release as possible. While there is no limit to the number and kinds of assets you can create, we recommend the following as a minimum:

- a release announcement
- a short, shareable book description (you likely have this already in your project scoping docs)
- blurbs or praise for the book
- a book cover
- several Tweet-length blurbs that can be cut and pasted

If you have the time, it can also be valuable to write up a short narrative about how the book was conceived and created, including a description of your experience during the process. Since publishing open textbooks is fairly unconventional, highlighting what distinguishes the production process is bound to attract some attention. It may even inspire others to follow in your footsteps! You can also create pamphlets, slide decks, or other marketing items, but only do what is feasible given your timelines and workload. For more inspiration, take a look at our Marketing and Communications overview.

Whatever assets you prepare, be sure to share them widely – on a blog or other web page, in key listservs, at major conferences, on social media, within your team, and in the Rebus Community platform. Ask others to spread the word, too, and keep the momentum up so that your release is on the radar for a few weeks. You may want to create a detailed promotional plan, with key dates and major events, so you can add momentum over the course of the release. If you do, share the plan with anyone helping out, so that everyone is on the same page.

EXECUTE THE PLAN, AND SAVOUR THE MOMENT!

Once you've completed the steps above, the only thing left to do is to execute your promotional plan and shout it from the rooftops. As this happens, build in some time for you and your team to celebrate the moment, and pat yourselves on the back for this incredible achievement. Creating an open textbook is no easy feat, but you've done it! Take it all in, and enjoy the calm, before thinking about any next steps.

START LOOKING AHEAD

As your book becomes part of the disciplinary landscape, and communities of practice around the world begin to adopt and adapt it, it may be time to think about a long-term vision for your book. Do you want to create ancillary materials? Is there a series to be created, or a revised edition to be planned? Should the book be translated into different languages? Try to engage the community around you in this planning – they may become part of a future project's leadership team.

NEED FURTHER ASSISTANCE?

We hope these suggestions will help you share your resource with the world. As we noted, we'll continue to add to this Guide as we work with more projects, and we welcome your ideas on what else we could add, or your feedback on how these approaches have worked (or not!) for you.

If you have questions, or anything to add, please let us know in the Rebus Community project home.

[Example] Proposed Formatting Workflow

This template may be used to define the process involved when transferring draft content into Pressbooks (or similar publishing tool). You can access an editable version of this example online.

FORMATTING WORKFLOW IN PRESSBOOKS

- Create Pressbooks shell, and select a theme to use in the book (some themes, like Malala, are explicitly designed for textbooks).
- Prepare a formatting guide or set up a chapter template (with all elements formatted) in Pressbooks. You could also use the first chapter as an example. Include instructions on:
  - nesting of headings
  - alternative text for images
  - sensible link text
  - media attributions
  - glossary items
  - interactive elements
  - tables
  - lists

- textboxes (learning outcomes, student tips)
- footnotes
- references

- Transfer a chapter into Pressbooks, using the docx Import tool or by copying and pasting from your draft document.

- Clean up content in the Text Editor (removing any <span> or <div> tags that might interfere with the default formatting from the theme).

- Check if anything has been lost in the transfer (links, heading hierarchy, lists, images, multimedia, etc.).

- Format the content as outlined in the formatting guide. Save your changes.

- Preview the content in web, PDF, EPUB. Make changes until the content looks satisfactory in each of these formats.

- If necessary, adjust the Theme Options on the book.

- Repeat 3-7 for the remaining chapters in the book (bulk import if necessary).

- Then add frontmatter and backmatter elements, and repeat 5-7.
  - Frontmatter:
    - Acknowledgements
    - Dedication
    - Introduction
    - How to use the book (for students or instructors)
    - What is an open textbook
    - Praise for the book
  - Backmatter:
    - References
    - Glossary

- Ancillaries (slides, answers to exercises/quizzes)
- Review statement
- Version History (including the publication date and version number of the first edition)
- Licensing and Attribution information
- Accessibility Assessment
- About the Contributors
- Feedback and Suggestions
- Adoption Form

- Enter the metadata in the Book Information. At minimum, input the:
  - Title
  - Short and long description
  - Subject
  - License
  - Team
  - Cover
  - Rebus project homepage link (so others can contact you or the team)
- At this stage, you may want to proofread the book or conduct accessibility review or classroom review. Do what's required and make necessary revisions to your content.
- Export files in web, editable, and offline formats, and conduct final checks for every format.
- Adjust the settings to allow these formats to be downloaded from the book homepage.
- Set up print-on-demand, if possible. Include a link to purchase a print copy in the book homepage.
- Notify the team and send them a link to view the book.

- Update Rebus project homepage with a link to the book.
- Execute your marketing plan to release the book.

 *This work is licensed under the Creative Commons Attribution 4.0 International License.*
Find an editable version of this template here.

[Example] Formatting Accessible Tables

This set of examples is used to illustrate common errors when formatting tables in Pressbooks, and how these can be fixed. These examples includes a information developed by *The Story of Earth: An Observational Guide* by Daniel Hauptvogel & Virginia Sisson. Our thanks to the team at Daniel Hauptvogel, Virginia Sisson, and their team.

ORIGINAL TABLES FROM "THE STORY OF EARTH"

In Table 1.1, the header cells are marked using bold formatting, instead of the scoping attribute. This makes it difficult for screen readers to process this information. Instead, we've reformatted the information in Table 1.3 to properly mark the header rows and columns.

Table 1.1 – Comparison of oceanic and continental crust.

Property	Oceanic Crust	Continental Crust
Thickness	7-10 km	25-80 km
Density	$3.0g/cm^3$	$2.7g/cm^3$
Silica (SiO_2) Content	50%	60%
Composition	Fe, Mg, and Ca silicates	K, Na, and Al silicates
Color	Dark	Light

In Table 1.2, the merged cells may prove difficult to read by a screen even if properly marked. So instead, reformat the table as shown in Table 1.4 and 1.5

Table 1.2 – Earthquake location data from Chile (from Martinod et al., 2010)

Chile-Peru Border		Central Chile	
Distance from trench (km)	Depth (km)	Distance from trench (km)	Depth (km)
200	30	170	40
220	50	220	65
300	65	400	90
370	125	200	50
500	190	120	20
300	100	500	110
250	65	350	85
210	40	300	75
280	80	250	60
450	175	280	75
400	140	200	55
410	150	260	90

REFORMATTED TABLES FOR IMPROVED ACCESSIBILITY

Table 1.3 – Comparison of oceanic and continental crust.

Property	Oceanic Crust	Continental Crust
Thickness	7-10 km	25-80 km
Density	$3.0 g/cm^3$	$2.7 g/cm^3$
Silica (SiO_2) Content	50%	60%
Composition	Fe, Mg, and Ca silicates	K, Na, and Al silicates
Color	Dark	Light

Table 1.4 – Earthquake location data from Chile-Peru Border (from Martinod et al., 2010)

Distance from trench (km)	Depth (km)

200	30
220	50
300	65
370	125
500	190
300	100
250	65
210	40
280	80
450	175
400	140
410	150

Table 1.5 – Earthquake location data from Central Chile (from Martinod et al., 2010)

Distance from trench (km)	Depth (km)
170	40
220	65
400	90
200	50
120	20
500	110
350	85
300	75
250	60
280	75
200	55
260	90

POST-RELEASE CONSIDERATIONS

Adoption Summary

Having your book adopted by an instructor for use in a given course is a vote of confidence about its overall quality and value to learners.

Whether or not adoption is the explicit goal you've been working towards, the open license on your book is nonetheless an indicator that you recognize that others can benefit from your book. It's therefore worth putting in some effort to encourage and track adoptions.

<table>
<tr><td align="center">Underlying principles</td></tr>
</table>

Recognize the implications of the open license. The openness of OER means a lot for students and instructors, including access and use with few or no barriers. At the same time, openness can make it hard to keep track of who's using the book.**Be transparent and consensual about the data you're collecting.** State explicitly what information you're asking for and how it may be used. Follow the guidelines in your region, so that adopters are comfortable and informed when submitting their details.

Spread the word far and wide. The larger the group of people who know about your book, the greater the likelihood of adoptions and reported adoptions.

Be responsive to grow the community of practice. Act on adopter and student feedback, and put adopters in touch with each other and the rest of the project team. Remain attentive to ways in which adopters can help expand and update the text.

Be flexible! Adopters might not follow your preferred methods of reporting, but it's still a win if they're using the book and letting you know!

Who's Involved?

The community around your book will grow with time, but to start it includes:

- Project manager: sets up Adoption Forms, submits reports about the book's impact, communicates with the group of adopters

- Authors: connect with potential adopters, can be adopters themselves, revise content based on feedback from adopters and students

- Editors: connect with potential adopters, can be adopters themselves, review feedback from adopters and students, decide which changes are immediate and which should wait for newer versions or editions of the book

- Reviewers: connect with potential adopters, can be adopters themselves

- Students: provide feedback about the book after using it in their classroom

- New Adopters: use the book in their classroom, join the community around the book, participate in revising or expanding the book

Key Tactics

While there are technical challenges in tracking how many people are using your book and in getting them to join your community, you can start with the following:

- Create a clear and simple Adoption Form that also explains why the information is being collected, how it may be used, and by whom.

- Ensure there are clear ways for adopters to find the form and communicate with the team.

- Keep a master spreadsheet of adopters.

- Poll all the existing team members to find out if they are going to use the book.

- Follow up regularly about the effect of the book on withdrawal and retention rates in classrooms.

- Introduce adopters to one another, and conduct conference calls during the semester about book usage.

- Get permission from adopters to use their names and affiliations, and any praise for the book, in promotional materials.

- Ask adopters to share their experience of using the book at conferences, in presentations, in their writing, on listservs, and elsewhere.

- Share ancillary materials with adopters and brainstorm with them about what else is needed to improve the book.

Not everyone who uses the book will want to engage with you and its community, including reporting their adoption. Not knowing the exact number of adopters may be a bit disappointing, so it's important to focus on the limitless use of the book you've enabled with its license and formats!

Read on to learn more about the whys and hows of adoption.

Adoption Overview

This part of *The Rebus Guide to Publishing Open Textbooks (So Far)* will take you through the life of the book following its Big Release and into its use in classrooms. Whether you've created an open textbook just for your classroom or for a much wider group of instructors, it's no doubt exciting, gratifying, and a little nerve-wracking to see the book adopted and put into action. In this section, we'll cover things like creating and using adoption forms, collecting feedback, tracking usage, and more. This section is mainly about how to find people to use your resource in their class, and engage with them; if you're looking for more instructions on how to design your course around an OER, keep an eye on expansions to the *Guide!*

As in the other sections of the *Guide*, these suggestions are based on our experience with open textbook projects. If you have questions about this overview, or suggestions for what else we should include, please share them in the Rebus Community project home. This document is an evolving draft, based on what we have learned so far in managing open textbook projects and gathering community feedback. We welcome your thoughts and contributions, including ways to improve the *Guide* overall.

THE SIGNIFICANCE OF ADOPTIONS

From having your open textbook used in a single section of a single course to seeing an entire university department incorporate it into all their classes, "adoption" can mean a variety of things. In our framing, having a resource adopted generally means that it has been assigned, either in part or in full, as part of the materials for a given course.

In any case, adoption is often the moment that you've been working for. Even if you embarked on this project simply to create a book for your own class or course, the fact that you decided to apply an open license to the book means that you've already been thinking of other educators and students that might benefit from your work in the long run. So, once you reach the point of releasing your book, it's worth it to put in a bit of effort to encourage and track adoptions.

Adoptions are an important measure of impact for a book for all sorts of reasons. Given the amount of time and effort you and your collaborators have put into it, it can be incredibly validating to see your book go out into the world and be used by others. Adoptions can also demonstrate the value of a text to your discipline, as it's a vote of confidence from adopters, and they also help validate the quality of the book, which in turn encourages more adoptions!

What's more, tracking adoptions is also important when it comes to showing the impact of OER at your institution, to your professional associations, in grant reports, and for future funding applications. These processes often require hard numbers to show value (for better or worse!), so if you do a little bit of work up front, you can have these numbers to hand when the time comes. The information you collect about adoptions is a powerful tool to make the case for OER, as it demonstrates the direct impact on students. This helps make the case for increased institutional investment in the creation of new OER and to the maintenance and further adoption of existing resources.

Lastly, adoptions are yet another extension of the theme of all open textbook publishing as we see it: collaboration! Everyone and anyone who is using the book, who benefits from this content being openly licensed, is an asset. By connecting with adopters, you can create more opportunities to gather feedback, new contributions, ideas, updates, spinoffs, ancillaries and more, and it all comes from people who are just as invested as you are in the book being maintained and improved in the long term. Each time the book is adopted, the community around it becomes larger. Making sure you can find those adopters (and they can find you!) can make all the difference in keeping a book alive over time.

THE BASICS OF GETTING AND TRACKING ADOPTIONS

As discussed in other sections of the *Guide*, a major portion of setting up feedback and reporting channels for adoption takes place during the release preparation. Even so, you can also start thinking about adoptions as early as content creation, editing, and review. Along the way to release, you have hopefully collected a list of people (and their email addresses!) who are interested in the book and have shown signs of wanting to adopt it when it is ready.

The main place to start is to set up an adoption form to track usage, and find out if anyone has already started using the book in their courses. Check out our Adoption Form as an example of what this form can look like (it can be modified to include more or less detail as needed). The best way to track adoptions is to ask users to self-report via the adoption form, so make sure this form is visible clearly from the book's home page, and that it is also in any major communications about the book, like the official announcement. Lastly, make sure to include clear pathways for communication, so adopters know how to contact you or other folks who are using the book. This can be as simple as a link to the Rebus Community project home, your email address, or other contact information.

Once the form has been set up, you can start promoting your book and encouraging educators to adopt it. An easy way to begin is to poll all your team members (contributors, volunteer, advisors etc.), asking if they might be interested in using the book now that it has been released and to fill out the form if so. You can also turn towards more traditional methods of soliciting adoptions, such as sharing the release announcement and some copies of the book with instructors or department heads. Following the big release, keep the noise and momentum around the book going by talking it up within your network, at conferences, and ask other members on your team and staff at your campus to do the same! Keep your resource's unique selling points in mind during these conversations, and also point to any additional items that could be packaged along with the book (such as slide decks, question banks, instructor workbooks, or other ancillaries) to motivate and attract people to adopt your book. Remember, the larger the group of people who know about your book, the higher the possibility of reported adoptions.

AFTER ADOPTIONS HAVE BEEN REPORTED

Ideally, you should set up the Adoption Form and communications pathways prior to releasing your book. Once you start receiving adoption reports, we recommend reaching out to these people, both to let them know how appreciative you are, and to build on the momentum. Gauge how interested they are in giving feedback, and do your best to bring them into the fold! (Some people will just want to use the book and not get involved, which is perfectly fine. Just make sure they have a clear line back to you if ever they need or want to use it, and you never know when they might show up again.)

For those who are keen, here are some ways to engage them:

- Put adopters in touch with one another, so that there are multiple lines of communication within the community of users.

- Conduct conference calls with the group, so that they can share observations and feedback about the book as they are teaching with it.

- Request permission to use their name and/or affiliation in your own reporting about adoptions.

- Request quotes from them about using the book, which can be added to promotional materials in order to inspire others to adopt the book as well.

- Ask each adopter to share their experience of using the book during conference presentations, in a blog post, on listserv messages, and within their networks.

- Share any ancillary materials with the group, or if none exist, brainstorm types that should be created, and ways to make them collaboratively.

Throughout, make sure you keep an eye on how adopters can help expand and update the text. This group of people believe in and are invested in your book, so they are more likely to be willing to help maintain and update it over time.

WHAT INFORMATION SHOULD YOU COLLECT, AND HOW?

We've found that it's best to start with a simple form, so that those responding aren't too overwhelmed. As you get more comfortable with the group of adopters over time, you can also ask them to provide more information about how the book is being used, building on the initial questions in your Adoption Form. Find the right balance between the full information you would like to have down the line and those details that you absolutely need up front.

Some information is easier to ask for outside of the form, too, so keep track of those questions (and why you are asking them) for when the right occasion arises. In the spirit of transparent and consensual data collection, it's important to be clear and explicit about the reasons you are collecting certain information. If possible, also tell them what you will be doing with it. For instance, if you're using the book in your course, you might want to get in touch with the folks on your campus who monitor information like student retention or withdrawal rates, and ask other adopters to do the same. With that kind of information collected, you can build the case for the relevance of your course, for a departmental adoption of your book, and for the increased use of OER. Telling your adopters the impact of the information that they share can help incentivize them to submit data and feel more comfortable doing so.

Another suggestion is to keeping an eye out for broader OER tracking projects, like SPARC's initiative to report USD $1 billion in student savings, and see what information might be required for these projects. Accordingly, update your own Adoption form or follow-up questions that you routinely send new adopters. You might also look at repositories that ask for adoption information, to either expand your form or find out if any adoptions of your book have been reported. For examples, see BCcampus' Adoption Form and their Open Textbook Statistics page.

Use whatever information you have available, whether it is data reported by adopters in the form, statistics from your institutional repository, statistics from other repositories, analytics from Pressbooks (or wherever your book is hosted), etc. In so doing, however, don't forget to also listen to adopter and student feedback about the book's content and structure. We have an entire section about improving your textbook, which includes what you can do with the feedback you receive. Ultimately, because tracking OER adoptions can't rely on the more conventional metric of unit sales, it will always be an issue of thinking creatively and paying attention to alternative forms and types of usage data.

CHALLENGES WITH TRACKING OPEN TEXTBOOK AND OER USE

While we've set out what we've found to be best practices tracking adoptions here, things will always play out a little differently than expected in practice. For a start, when it comes to the data you collect, changing or adding metrics to your original Adoption Form over time, either based on your own needs, or what you've seen others collect, can result in a messy data set. You may need to contact those who filled out older versions of the form, asking them to provide additional information. It is an extra step for both of you, but generally worth it for the data!

As well, be ready to collect information in other ways. Although you may have set up clear pathways to your adoption form (or other data-collection mechanism), it may be that adopters will end up contacting you via email or your Rebus Community project home. Make sure you record this information in a master spreadsheet. Even if they didn't use your preferred methods to communicate this information, it's still a win that they are using the book!

Keep in mind, too, that you might come across some adopters who are not interested in engaging with the community or contributing a lot of information. Don't try to force them to share or do more than they are willing. Not everyone has the time or energy or interest to be an active member of the adopter group, and that's okay. Thank them for being interested in the resource, and continue to update them as the book lives on. (You may win them over down the road.)

And finally, remember that one of the best things about your book is also what makes it hard to keep track of who's using it. Sharing your work as a web-native resource (we hope!) with an open license means it can be hard to know exactly who is using it, where, and how. Anyone can have access to your book's website, or download it in different formats, without barriers – which is a good thing! But while this kind of openness is a big part of the power of OER, and opens up all kinds of exciting possibilities, it also poses a challenge to assessing how the resource is being used. Think of it this way: the same barriers that traditionally limit access to books are also the most accurate ways to collect information about how a book is being used (think sales, account logins etc.).

With fewer barriers to access in place, open textbook creators have to rely on self-reporting by adopters. Many will happily do so, but some won't, for all sorts of reasons. It might be due to lack of clarity about the adoption form, not know the form exists, lack of time or attention, or a lack of incentive or motivation. While it can be a bit annoying to not know the exact number of people using your book (or to not even know if you know or not), take pride in the limitless use you've enabled with the license and formats! There's something very exciting about sharing your work without knowing exactly where and how it will be used. Moreover, you won't be alone in feeling frustrated – everyone in the OER community is with you! Solutions to this issue are in the works, and if you have any suggestions to offer based on your experiences collecting adoption information, let us know in the Rebus Community project home!

Ultimately, even if you did everything possible to set yourself up for success to track adoptions and engage adopters, it may not happen the way you want. This is okay – your book is a gift, and what matters is that it is available and accessible to all those who want or need it.

NEED FURTHER ASSISTANCE?

We hope these suggestions will help you keep track of how your resource is being used around the world. We'll continue to add to the *Guide* as we work with more projects, and we welcome your ideas on what else we might add, as well as your feedback on how these approaches have worked (or not!) for you.

If you have questions, or anything to add, please let us know in the Rebus Community project home.

Improvements and Maintenance Summary

Every book should have an 'afterlife' beyond its initial use — changing and evolving to ensure ongoing relevance and continued adoption. Regardless of whether your resource is web-based or printed, it will need some amount of editorial attention in order to remain valuable.

In this way, your role shifts from creation to a focus on maintenance, updates, corrections, and planning or coordinating future versions and editions.

> ### Underlying principles
>
> **Maintain the resource so as to strengthen it and improving its perception.** Books that are not updated can be seen as out of date and therefore not be considered seriously by potential adopters.
>
> **Be responsive to changes in theory, discourse, and practice.** Corrections, updates, and additions can be based on reviewer and adopter feedback, as well as wider shifts in the book's discipline or subject area.
>
> **Be public about in-progress and completed updates.** Anyone invested in the resource will be motivated to keep it up to date; informing them about expected improvements can prompt them to help or simply look forward to the update.
>
> **Carefully time when you carry out changes.** Although making changes to

OER is relatively easy and flexible, be considerate towards current users of the book. Updates in the middle of a semester or teaching period can have a disruptive impact on learning.

Parse, process, and plan before you do. Prioritize which tasks need completing first, based on the resources at hand and the complexity of the tasks. Use the scale of changes to determine timelines and the release of new versions and editions.

Who's Involved?

The possibilities of improvements, spinoffs, and adaptations are endless, but they don't all need to be done by you alone. Reach out to the rest of the team!

- Project managers: coordinate and notify teams about similar projects, make connections between new and current collaborators, oversee projects through to completion

- Authors: implement changes, record them in the Version History

- Editors: prioritize work for future versions or editions, implement changes, record them in the Version History

- Adopters: assist with implementing changes, take charge of a spinoff project

- New collaborators: assist with implementing changes, take charge of a spinoff project

- Adapters: share improvements back to the original book, implement changes, lead new adaptation projects

Key Tactics

Whether the changes you are working on are new, or were planned earlier in the project but never executed, keep the following in mind:

- Look for grammatical errors, broken links, and accessibility of formats.
- Find newly created OER repositories and submit your book for inclusion.
- Make small maintenance changes to the webbook anytime during the year.
- Only make larger additions or updates to the webbook and other formats during breaks in academic sessions.
- Look for trends or shifts in your discipline or subject area, and make updates that reflect and respond to them.
- List error reports and corrections publicly.
- Record larger changes, like edits, additions, updates, and expansions in the Version History.
- Indicate new versions by point increments (e.g., from version 1.2 to version 1.3) and new editions by whole number increases (e.g., from edition 1 to edition 2)
- Add ancillaries, new formats, and media—another type of improvement that moves beyond simple corrections.
- Contact the team and collaborators, including adopters, to help as needs arise.
- Set up clear communication pathways from the book and ancillaries, so new collaborators can reach out.
- Identify an interim project manager if you need to step away or share the workload.
- Always keep everyone informed about ongoing work and estimated timeframes for completion.

Part of what makes open textbooks important is the community building that goes hand-in-hand with their creation. This doesn't stop when the book is released, so continue to gather people together as you plan updates, and encourage them to add to or modify the resource as it suits their needs.

Keep reading to learn more about maintaining and improving your open textbook.

Improvements and Maintenance Overview

This part of *The Rebus Guide to Publishing Open Textbooks (So Far)* will take you through the 'afterlife' of your book, and its journey beyond use in classrooms. The release and adoption of your open textbook are big milestones worth celebrating, but they also mark the beginning of a new set of steps. As a living document, your book will continue to change and evolve, and so will your role as creator. Your efforts now shift to maintenance, updates, corrections, and the planning and coordination of future versions.

In this section of the *Guide*, we cover things like following up on errata reports, updating formats, more substantive improvements and additions, and more.

As in other sections, these suggestions are based on our experience with open textbook projects to date. If you have questions about this overview, or suggestions for what else we should include, please share them in the Rebus Community project home. This document is an evolving draft, and continually incorporates community feedback. We welcome your thoughts and contributions, including ways to improve the *Guide* overall.

WHY CARE ABOUT YOUR TEXTBOOK BEYOND RELEASE?

Once your OER is released, it's understandable that you would want to savour the moment, to enjoy the book's existence in the world and to celebrate having completed a huge piece of work! Nonetheless, while the bulk of of your efforts is complete, it's important to remember that *maintaining* the book is important — to ensure its ongoing relevance and continued adoption.

Books, regardless of whether they are web-based or printed, need some amount of editorial attention to remain valuable resources. This maintenance includes gathering feedback from adopters and readers, which is is invaluable for strengthening the text. It's also necessary, because you will never be able to catch every single typo in the book prior to release, and because you will need to routinely check for broken links, among other changes that are out of your control.

A book that is not improved, updated, and maintained can be perceived as being 'too old' and 'out-of-date' very quickly and therefore not seriously considered as an option by educators seeking course materials. In a way, a book's usefulness can depend on the amount of attention that it receives – as people see news of updates, changes, or improvements to the book, they will be more likely to peruse the book and use it in their course!

WHAT MAINTENANCE ENTAILS

Maintaining an open textbook doesn't need to be a complicated matter. As we see it, maintenance includes ongoing changes that are more about function than content, made at any point, during the academic year. This entails keeping tabs on the book with an eye to grammatical errors, typos, or broken links. You may also choose to track and respond to any error reports that readers and adopters of the book have submitted (including thanking them for their keen eyes, and perhaps asking if they want to get involved with other improvements!)

If your resource is hosted on the web, part of the maintenance process should involve ensuring that it is still accessible in its web format along with other offline and editable formats. And to ensure maximum distribution, find out if any new OER repositories have been created since the book's initial release, and then make sure you submit it for inclusion there.

Further down, we get into more detail about the timing, order, and significance of different type of maintenance revisions.

IMPROVEMENTS AND ADDITIONS

While "maintenance" refers to smaller, ongoing changes to an open textbook, we call more significant changes to content "improvements and additions." These are made at particular moments following the book's release, unlike the more frequent and unscheduled corrections that are part of maintenance. These changes can be split into three categories:

- qualitative improvements to existing content
- quantitative additions to existing content
- disciplinary or thematic updates

Following adoption and classroom use of the book, you are bound to receive different forms of constructive feedback regarding the content. For instance, you may have been told that a particular unit has proven to be very difficult for students to understand, or that specific elements like case studies, exercises, or references are not as clear as they should be.

These constitute opportunities for improving those parts of the resource, which should be done during this phase in the book's life-cycle. Improvements can also be implemented based on feedback from reviewers—those issues that were not addressed during the initial creation of the book. It's also critical in this phase to revisit and resolve outstanding accessibility issues, as well as new ones that have been identified as the book has been used.

During this stage, you can also make additions to the content. These may include elements that were initially planned for inclusion but didn't make it into the first release, suggestions from reviewers, proposals from adopters, and ideas you and your team came up with post-release. Additions can also come in the form of ancillary materials, like slide decks, question banks, exercises, and other supplementary content. We go into more detail about ancillary materials in later sections of the *Guide*, so keep reading!

The last category of revisions are those that become relevant due to changes within the textbook's discipline or subject area, or in response to real-world changes that provide new or improved examples of theoretical concepts. It is particularly important to split out this category from improvements and additions, as it highlights how OER can be responsive to wider changes theory, discourse, and practice. For this part of the process, pay attention to these larger themes, including examples, case studies, language and terminology, methodologies that are cited, resource lists, and literature reviews.

All of these changes should be included in the book's Version History, which serves as a record of the various changes, edits, additions, and updates that are made over time. Take a look at our version history template and adapt it as needed for your book.

TIMING AND PROCESS

Depending on the extent of improvements, additions, and updates to be made, they will need to be carried out at different times after release. A major concern, therefore, is the impact that making changes during the school year will have on students and teachers who are using the book in their courses. This includes the changes made to different formats of the book too, as students will be accessing the book in a variety of ways (on the web, in other digital formats like EPUB, PDF, MOBI, and as printed copies).

The upshot is that *maintenance* changes (correcting typos, broken links, etc.) are the only type of revisions we advise making during the school year, and these should only be made to the web-based version of the resource. Changes to the print version and other formats will need to wait for a pause in the academic year or until year-end, depending on how the in-school time is organized in your region. Each maintenance change does not need to be marked as a new edition of the book, nor does it necessarily require comprehensive tracking in the Version History. We do recommend, however, that error reports and corrections be listed publicly, so readers can see what those changes are and note them in their teaching and learning contexts, as well as avoid submitting duplicate error reports. Take a look at some example errata lists from OpenStax, along with examples of how to share these lists in printed PDF formats, and some inspirations for the errata form itself.

For other improvements and updates, we suggest that you first parse and process the extent of the changes needed, and then plan out a timeline to do so. Some changes may be easier or harder to implement, or require less or more participation from the team. As you're deciding on your tasks and timeline, also think through who will make these changes and assign the right people to them. The scale of changes, from classroom feedback to significant additions planned by the team, will determine whether a new edition or a new version of the book will need to be released (more on this below). The important thing is to be responsive to adopters, readers, and other scholars, and clearly surface the changes that you are making to the text in the version history.

When significant changes have been made and there is a new version or edition of your resource, inform all of its known adopters before replacing the old format of the book. And if possible, inform everyone of the specific updates, additions, corrections that have been made— either by pointing to the Version History, or to a list of improvements (if it is a new edition). See an example of this in *Media Innovation and Entrepreneurship*.

EDITIONS AND VERSIONS

The differences between a new version of a textbook and a new edition of a textbook bear clarification. As we think of it, a new *version* contains only minor changes – maintenance and smaller-scale improvements to the existing content. A new *edition* of the book incorporates major changes to content, such as additions and updates to the original release.

New versions of a book are usually indicated by point increments (e.g., 1.1, 1.2, 1.3, …), while new editions are indicated by whole number increases (e.g., 1st edition, 2nd edition, 3rd edition, …) The release of a new edition is a time to rally more attention within and beyond your community, and perhaps some promotional efforts as well. If this is the case, do so strategically, and only if the revisions merit it. If there have only been subtle changes and updates, it may not warrant extensive promotion.

Releases of new editions can sometimes be disruptive, especially if they happen frequently (every year, for instance), as students might be working with older physical copies of the book that are more easily available and/ or affordable. While one of the many advantages of publishing openly is the flexibility and ease of making changes, it is still important to be considerate towards ongoing users of the book, bearing in mind the impact that changes will have on them.

If you are working on a new edition of your book, be public about it, and communicate in advance with your team and adopters about the expected changes and updates. Doing so lets them know what is coming, and may even motivate some people to help you make these improvements. Once the changes have been completed, reach out and update everyone, pointing to the new edition and Version History that clearly outlines updates you have made.

SPINOFFS AND SIDE PROJECTS

So far, we've only addressed updates and improvements to the core textbook, but there are other ways in which you may like to expand on your book. Ancillary materials like slide decks, question banks, instructor manuals, and student workbooks can supplement your resource and make it a more appealing package for adopters. You can begin work on these projects following the book's release, or if you have the resources to do so, concurrent to the book's production!

With the open license on your book, the different types of spinoffs are endless. For instance, translations, spelling conversions (eg.: American to British spelling), or cultural adjustments can make it accessible for use in more regions. Other adaptations, small or large, can make the text work better in different pedagogical contexts, or incorporate regionally specific content that makes it relevant to a different set of users, thus expanding the pool of readers around your book.

While adaptations mostly maintain consistency of the content, other variants like **remixing** can involve blending content from the book with other openly licensed content. For example, *Blueprint for Success in College and Career* remixes sections from four other OER: *Foundations of Academic*

Success, A Different Road to College: A Guide for Transitioning Non-traditional Students, How to Learn Like a Pro!, and *College Success.*

Other ways to build on your book is to think of new formats and media through which to share content. You could create an audiobook version of the text, a series of short videos summarizing each unit, or a poster series that creates visualizations of the content. The possibilities are endless!

WHO MAKES THESE CHANGES?

As we've seen so far, there's a lot that you can do to maintain and improve on your already carefully crafted open textbook! The main thing to keep in mind that all these improvements do not need to be made by you alone. In fact, it probably won't and can't all be done by you – and that's a good thing. Part of what makes creating open textbooks important is the community building that goes hand in hand. This doesn't stop with the book's release, but continues during improvements and maintenance. Keep gathering people around the book during this phase, from adopters to adapters, so that both the book and the community can grow with time!

The first source of help for maintenance and improvements is the team and collaborators who were involved in creating the resource. Reach out to them as needs arise, and you may be surprised at their response! You can also reach out to the people who are using the book – adopters may well be very motivated to help make changes, as they are the ones who directly benefit from improvements to the book.

Simply put, any individual or organization invested in the value of the resource has an incentive to contribute to maintaining it and keeping it up-to-date in the long term. Depending on the type of project or work that is being done to improve or add to the book, you may even find funders willing to invest financially, or others who can secure budgets through institutional, local, or state grants.

For this to happen, it is vital that you have clear communications pathways set up from your book and its ancillaries. That way, anyone who is interested in contributing in some way knows how to contact you or another team member. And if you find that you need to step away from the project at some point, make sure you've identified and involved someone else to take over or manage things in the interim. Look to your leadership team for this, because there will likely be someone who is eager and willing to take on the mantle.

And lastly, do what you can to be public about the status of the book, of other projects, and of changes, even if it's in the form of a short notice in the book or in your team's public discussion space. Leave the possibilities for the book open – and watch eagerly how they unfurl!

NEED FURTHER ASSISTANCE?

We hope these suggestions will help you maintain your textbook and follow its life and journey around the world. We'll continue to add to the *Guide* as we work with more projects, and we welcome your ideas on what else we might add, as well as your feedback on how these approaches have worked (or not!) for you.

If you have questions, or anything to add, please let us know in the Rebus Community project home.

Adaptations Summary

Adaptations mark the beginning of a new set of steps (and lives) for your open textbook. As people make substantial alterations to the resource, they create a stand-alone "fork" of it. This expands the potential reach and use of the book for new audiences, contexts, regions, and languages.

Underlying principles

Adaptation is openness in action. It's easier and more collectivist to create a new resource by building on one that already exists. The freedom to do so with open texts is distintinctive and rarely possible with conventional All Rights Reserved textbooks.

As open as possible and as closed as necessary. While there's no single license that's right for all creators, give back to the ecosystem by selecting the most permissive license that works for your project.

Boundless opportunities for customization. Adaptation projects can range from small-scale to very large in scope. In both cases, adapters should reshape the resource to fit their exact needs.

Modularity makes everything easier. A clear, consistent structure across your book, including a common template for each chapter, not only makes it better for learners, but also helps adapters swap in and out some elements of your text while keeping others in place.

Give what you get. Help grow the community of practice around the book with your adaptation, and do what's needed to track adaptations, demonstrate the book's impact, and maintain and improve the adaptation over time.

Who's Involved?

There are two sides to adaptation: one is setting up the original book so it can be easily adaptable, and the other is embarking on a new adaptation project. Many different people can be involved:

- Project manager: coordinates with new adapters and connects them with the team, tracks adaptations, collects corrections from adapters, encourages editorial and authoring teams to think about modular content

- Adopters: use new adaptations, start new adaptation projects

- Adapters: start new adaptation projects, submit changes back to the original book, join the community of practice, check permissions and licenses

- Authors: use new adaptations, create modular content, join adaptation projects

- Editors: check permissions and licensing, assist with the creation of modular content, join adaptation projects

- Reviewers: joins adaptation projects

- Marketing and communications: shares new adaptation projects, promotes demonstrable impact and success of adaptations

Key Tactics

Creating an adaptation that stands alone from the original book (or setting out the pathway for others to do so) is no small feat, but you can get going with these suggestions:

- Select a license that is as permissive as possible.

- Make your book available in at least one editable format.

- Support modularity by referring to chapters by titles not numbers, and by keeping context-specific information separate from theory or concepts.

- Create a backmatter section that gives adapters a reference for content-specific information in your book, as well as permissions or licensing information of elements.

- Provide sample messaging for attribution, which adapters and adopters can use to give their thanks to you and your team.

- Request that adapters remove the attribution if you do not want to be associated with the adapted version.

- Track adaptations by asking adapters to self-report.

- Clearly indicate how adapters can connect with you and the community.

- Join forces and collaborate with others who are already underway with adaptation projects.

- Consult the backmatter sections of books for permissions and licensing information.

- Adopt a license that meets the features of the original book's license, or consult with copyright librarians about fair-use or fair-dealing rules in your region.

- Define the differences between the adaptation and the original book, on the book's homepage, in front matter, or in the metadata.

- Provide links from the original book to the adaptation and vice versa.

- Update the original creators about your adaptation project's progress.

- Generate buzz around your book and community with the added value that an adaptation provides.

Ultimately, adaptations are a measure of the value of the book to its discipline, to educators, and to students. Stay proud of the opportunities that your open textbook creates, and use this kind of work to encourage more adoptions of the book and to boost your professional profile!

Keep reading to learn more about how to set up or create adaptations.

Adaptations Overview

This final part of *The Rebus Guide to Publishing Open Textbooks (So Far)* takes you through the considerations around adapting an open textbook, including the benefits of adaptation, enabling adaptations, and other best practices. Like adoptions, adaptations also mark the beginning of a new set of steps (and new lives) for your open textbook.

As in other sections, these suggestions are based on our experience with open textbook projects to date. If you have questions about this overview, or suggestions for what else we should include, please share them in the Rebus Community project home. This document is an evolving draft, and continually incorporates community feedback. We welcome your thoughts and contributions, including ways to improve the *Guide* overall.

WHAT IS ADAPTATION?

Broadly speaking, adaptation means making changes to an existing resource. Unlike creating a new open textbook, adaptation involves working with an existing text, and also relates to making more conceptual or substantial alterations to a book, so that it can better suit your needs as an teacher.

Adaptations can serve to localize the book to your specific region, to customize it for your class, to translate it for increased use, or to make the book accessible in a different format (e.g., an audiobook). All these instances involve creating a "project fork," that is, another version of the text that can stand alone and separate from the original book or work. Accordingly, adaptations need to be maintained and updated on their own, in parallel to the way that the creators of the original work have to ensure their book's upkeep and continued use.

BENEFITS OF ADAPTATION

Adaptations are a great demonstration of the advantages of open licenses that permit reuse, remixing, and redistribution. Because it is sometimes easier to create a new resource by building on content that already exists, openly licensed texts are invaluable.

Adaptation also allows content to be shaped to better suit a variety of needs, from those of instructors and students, to the requirements of universities and individual courses. This level of freedom is distinctive of open texts, and is rarely available with conventionally All Rights Reserved books, which carry more restrictions on reusing and remixing content.

Adaptation also presents an opportunity to improve on the text by correcting errors or changing insensitive content. For instance, if your textbook contained inappropriate content, you can immediately make corrections to the web version. Not only is it this simple, but you could do so without affecting other sections, chapters, images, etc. At the end of the academic semester, you can conveniently apply this change to all the other formats, including print.

One of the other major benefits of adaptation is that it represents an opportunity to generate additional value around the book. Because it is not a static or isolated process, it can be abuzz with communication, conversation, and collaboration, growing the community around the original book and allowing new people to discover its potential expansions!

SETTING UP FOR EASIER ADAPTATION

If you're creating an open textbook, there are a number of ways that you can structure it to enable others to easily adapt your work. (We've mentioned the following suggestions previously in this *Guide*, so don't worry if you're already near the end of your book's creation.)

The first and possibly most important way to enable adaptation of your book is by choosing an open license. We encourage selecting a license that is as permissive as possible, understanding that there's no single open license that works for all creators. Try to be as open as possible and as closed as necessary with the license on your work. Ultimately, the open publishing ecosystem is one in which everybody benefits from the work that we all put in: keep this in mind when it comes to your own project.

In a similar vein, make sure that your book is available in at least one editable format when released, so adapters can reuse and repurpose the content without too much difficulty. A variety of editable formats is even better, giving adapters more options when it comes to pulling content from the book and remixing it.

As you're creating your content, try to do so in ways that make it modular. Part of this is to ensure that you have a clear and consistent structure across your book, so each chapter or unit follows a similar formula. Think about how units can be combined in different orders (that is, different from the one you have outlined yourself), or even stand alone and be used separate from the text. A simple way to assist future adapters of the text is to title and refer to chapters and units by name (not number). That way, if the adapter decides to reorder units, or only use some units, they are not bound by a numerical naming system. We also suggest that context-specific information, such as local examples, laws from your region of governance, statistics from your country or state organizations, etc., be modular, so that it too can be extracted from other content in the unit, to then be easily modified in the adaptation.

The back matter of your book is a good location to list places in the book that contain context-specific information, giving adapters quick reference. You can also clearly state permissions and licensing information here, including elements in the book that contain a license that is different from the book's global license. This section can also contain a few lines of sample messaging for attribution, so adapters know how you and other creators would like to be attributed in the adapted work. This information can be helpful for adopters and adapters alike. Take a look at the Licensing & Remixing Information in *Media Innovation and Entrepreneurship* for an example.

TRACKING ADAPTATIONS

It can also prove helpful to keep track of the different adaptations that are made—those that you are aware of. While this can be hard to do, creating even a small list of projects that are using your book is a way for the book's community to be aware of the work that is being done and possibly participate in it themselves! To help make this happen, give adapters clear pathways to contact you or the book's community. If possible, also share pathways for adapters to submit changes back to the original book, in case they catch any errors as they making their adaptations.

Keeping track of adaptations is a good way to measure your book's impact on the field, and in turn boost your professional profile. Just as you can track and communicate news about adoptions, adaptations are another measure of success.

Keeping an eye on adaptations is also useful if and when you come across a version that doesn't sit well with you or the team. As the original creators, you have the right to be attributed on adaptations, but you can also request that adapters *remove* your attribution if you prefer not to be associated with their work. While we hope this is not a request you would have to make often, it can be applied if need be.

HOW TO ADAPT AN OPEN TEXTBOOK

If you find yourself on the other side of the equation, and are adapting an existing open textbook, we have some basic tips for you too. First, it's always wise to check around to see if the type of adaptation you had in mind is already underway or completed. If you find that someone has started to create what you wanted, you can join forces and collaborate with them to avoid duplicating efforts. Even if no one is making a similar adaptation, putting out feelers for other adapters helps build community around the book.

Another practical step as you start out is to check the license of the book and make sure you have permission to adapt it in the way that you would like to. It's also good to check the license of individual elements in the book, like multimedia elements, since these can sometimes be licensed differently that the book as a whole. If the creator has a back matter section listing the book's permissions, licensing, and remixing information, be sure to consult it.

If you're not able to determine the license on the book or an individual element, we recommend you assume an "All Rights Reserved" license. In this case, consult the fair use or fair dealing laws in your region. These govern reasonable reuse of portions of the book within an adaptation. If you need assistance, consult the copyright librarians at your institution, if present, or ask for help from the community of practitioners in the Rebus Community platform.

As an adapter, make sure you select a license that complies with the license on the original book. For instance, if the original work is licensed with the Creative Commons Attribution ShareAlike license (CC-BY-SA), you are obligated to also license your adaptation CC-BY-SA. Be sure to credit the original authors in your adaptation, using the suggested wording if it is available. It's a nice gesture to also include a note in the front matter of your book, stating that your adaptation draws on one or more openly licensed books. See an example of this in the front matter of *Blueprint for Success*.

When it comes to doing the work of adapting, remember that it doesn't just have to be you—you can form a team around the project and make this a collaborative effort! Reach back to the original creators, not only to let them know that you are working on this project, but to see if they or others on the team can help. Once this line of communication is established, you can use it to feed back any corrections to the original text, in the case that you come across errors.

You should also chat with the original creator to clearly define the differences between your adaptation and the original work. Of course, this is something you and your team may have already defined, early on. Make sure that these differences are stated clearly, either in the front matter of your book, or perhaps in the book's description or metadata. That way, anyone coming across your book will also know whether the original work (or another adaptation) might work better for their course.

From there, they can then make the appropriate comparisons of the book in a repository or referatory. You can also provide links back to the original work, so it is more easily discoverable. This might encourage the creators to also include links to your adaptation in the original book. You get what you give!

We also recommend taking a look at BCcampus Open Education's *Adaptation Guide* for a more comprehensive guide to adapting an open textbook. And of course, take another look at the other sections of this *Guide* with adaptation in mind! The principles, examples, recommendations, and templates we provide have been written with a variety of projects in mind, so you can always refer to them as you move forward with adaptation.

NEED FURTHER ASSISTANCE?

We hope these suggestions will help, either as you make your book more easily adaptable or as you work to adapt an existing textbook. We'll continue to add to the *Guide* as we work with more projects. In the meantime, we welcome your ideas on what else we might add, as well as your feedback on how these approaches have worked (or not!) for you.

If you have questions, or anything to add, please let us know in the Rebus Community project home.

Making Open Textbooks: A Video Guide

If you're looking for a light overview of OER creation, check out the video series version of this guide. *Making Open Textbooks: A Video Guide* provides a brief summary of each of the major phases of creation. The short videos present the roles, models, and guidelines that make up the process of creating and publishing open textbooks. From project conception and rounding up a team of collaborators, to creating, editing, and reviewing your content, all the way through to release, marketing, adoptions, and revisions, these videos summarize the many steps along the way.

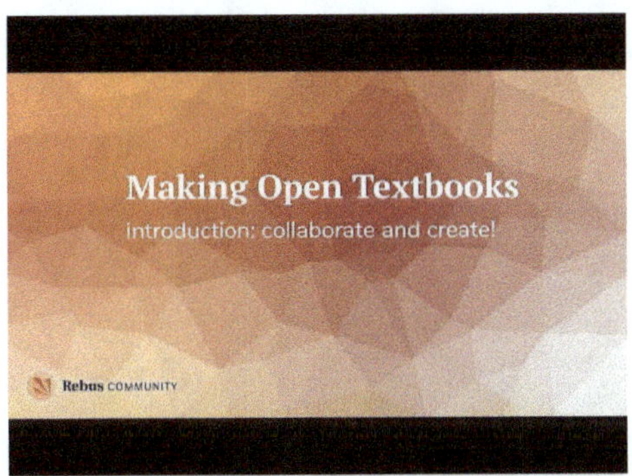

A YouTube element has been excluded from this version of the text. You can view it online here: https://press.rebus.community/the-rebus-guide-to-publishing-open-textbooks/?p=368

Making Open Textbooks: A Video Guide features Zoe Wake Hyde. It is edited and directed by David Szanto. Transcript and captions provided by Mei Lin.

Feedback and Suggestions

We are actively and enthusiastically soliciting feedback from instructors, faculty, administrators, OER program managers, librarians, instructional designers, students, and others using this book. You can leave feedback and suggestions in the Rebus Community project home at https://www.rebus.community/c/open-textbooks-in-development/the-rebus-guide-to-publishing.

About the Team

AUTHORS

Apurva Ashok studied literature and marketing at McGill University and completed the Master of Publishing program at Simon Fraser University. Her experience ranges across academic publishing, media, social justice, and volunteer work. In 2015, she co-founded *Harf*, a student-run journal on South Asian studies. Apurva strongly believes in translating knowledge across places and people and in the value of greater critical thinking for all.

Zoe Wake Hyde worked in media communications and academic administration in New Zealand before completing the Master of Publishing program at Simon Fraser University. Having gained an alternative view of academic publishing, she is now focused on creating value-exchange systems that support better, more democratic access to knowledge and learning.

EDITORS

David Szanto has worked in a number of different professions, including book publishing, new product and service development, innovation consulting, film finance, marketing-communications, and academia.

CONTRIBUTORS

Elizabeth Mays is director of sales and marketing for PressbooksEDU and an adjunct professor at the Walter Cronkite School of Journalism and

Mass Communication at Arizona State University. Previously she served as marketing manager at the Rebus Community and as an assistant director at Arizona State University. She is the editor of *A Guide to Making Open Textbooks With Students* and the co-editor of *Media Innovation & Entrepreneurship*, both of which were collaboratively built works published by the Rebus Community.

Accessibility Assessment

A NOTE FROM THE REBUS COMMUNITY

We are working to create a new, collaborative model for publishing open textbooks. Critical to our success in reaching this goal is to ensure that all books produced using that model meet the needs of all those who will one day use them. To us, open means inclusive, so for a book to be open, it must also be accessible.

As a result, we are working with accessibility experts and others in the OER community to develop best practices for creating accessible open textbooks, and are building those practices into the Rebus model of publishing. By doing this, we hope to ensure that all books produced using the Rebus Community are accessible by default, and require an absolute minimum of remediation or adaptation to meet any individual reader's needs.

While we work on developing guidelines and implementing support for authoring accessible content, we are making a good faith effort to ensure that books produced with our support meet accessibility standards wherever possible, and to highlight areas where we know there is work to do. It is our hope that by being transparent on our current books, we can begin the process of making sure that accessibility is top of mind for all authors, adopters, students, and contributors of all kinds on all our open textbook projects.

Below is a short assessment of eight key areas that have been assessed during the production process. The checklist has been drawn from the

BCcampus Open Education Accessibility Toolkit. While a checklist such as this is just one part of a holistic approach to accessibility, it is one way to begin our work on embedded good accessibility practices in the books we support.

Wherever possible, we have identified ways in which anyone may contribute their expertise to improve the accessibility of this text.

We also welcome any feedback from anyone who encounters the book and identifies an issue that needs resolving. This book is an ongoing project and will be updated as needed. If you would like to submit a correction or suggestion, please do so using the Rebus Community Accessibility Suggestions form.

ACCESSIBILITY CHECKLIST

Checklist for Accessibility in Webbook

Area of Focus	Requirements	Pass?
Organizing Content	Content is organized under headings and subheadings	Yes
Organizing Content	Headings and subheadings are used sequentially (e.g. Heading 1. Heading 2, etc.) as well as logically (if the title if Heading 1 then there should be no other Heading 1 styles as the title is the uppermost level)	Yes
Images	Images that convey information include Alternative Text (alt-text) descriptions of the image's content or function	Not Applicable
Images	Graphs, charts, and maps also include contextual or supporting details in the text surrounding the image	Not Applicable
Images	Images do not rely on colour to convey information	Yes
Images	Images that are purely decorative contain empty alternative text descriptions. (Descriptive text is unnecessary if the image doesn't convey contextual content information)	Yes
Tables	Tables include row and column headers	Yes

Tables	Tables include a title or caption	Yes
Tables	Tables do not have merged or split cells	Yes
Tables	Tables have adequate cell padding	Yes
Weblinks	The weblink is meaningful in context, and does not use generic text such as "click here" or "read more"	Yes
Weblinks	Weblinks do not open new windows or tabs	Yes
Weblinks	If weblinks must open in a new window, a textual reference is included in the link information	Not Applicable
Embedded Multimedia	A transcript has been made available for a multimedia resource that includes audio narration or instruction*	Yes
Embedded Multimedia	Captions of all speech content and relevant non-speech content are included in the multimedia resource that includes audio synchronized with a video presentation	Yes
Embedded Multimedia	Audio descriptions of contextual visuals (graphs, charts, etc.) are included in the multimedia resource	Not Applicable
Formulas	Formulas have been created using MathML	Yes
Formulas	Formulas are images with alternative text descriptions, if MathML is not an option	Not Applicable
Font Size	Font size is 12 point or higher for body text	Yes
Font Size	Font size is 9 point for footnotes or endnotes	Yes
Font Size	Font size can be zoomed to 200%	Yes

*Transcript includes:

- Speaker's name
- All speech content
- Relevant descriptions of speech

- Descriptions of relevant non-speech audio
- Headings and subheadings

Licensing Information

This book is licensed under a Creative Commons Attribution 4.0 license except where otherwise noted.

This license allows for reuse, adaptation, remixing, and redistribution of content, so long as you attribute it to the original authors, indicate if changes are made, and link to the original, free content, found at https://press.rebus.community/the-rebus-guide-to-publishing-open-textbooks/.

PLEASE CREDIT US AS FOLLOWS:

Redistributing the book verbatim:

This guide is created by Apurva Ashok and Zoe Wake Hyde, edited by David Szanto, and produced with support from the Rebus Community. The original is freely available under the terms of the CC BY 4.0 license at https://press.rebus.community/the-rebus-guide-to-publishing-open-textbooks/.

Revised or adapted versions:

This work is based on original content created by Apurva Ashok and Zoe Wake Hyde, edited by David Szanto, and produced with support from the Rebus Community. The original is freely available under the terms of the CC BY 4.0 license at https://press.rebus.community/the-rebus-guide-to-publishing-open-textbooks/.

Individual chapters or pieces:

Version History

This page provides a record of edits and changes made to this book since its initial publication. Whenever edits or updates are made in the text, we provide a record and description of those changes here. If the change is minor, the version number increases by 0.1. If the edits involve substantial updates, the edition number increases to the next whole number.

The files posted alongside this book always reflect the most recent version. If you find an error in this book, please let us know in the Rebus Community project home.

Version History

Version	Date	Change
1.0	October 2018	Original
2.0	30 September 2019	Second edition published, with updated book information and metadata. It includes the following additions: • 4 Steps to Starting an Open Textbook Project • Acknowledgements • Introduction • Praise for 'The Rebus Guide to Publishing Open Textbooks (So Far)' • Building a Team Summary • Project Scoping Summary • Authoring and Content Creation Summary • Editing Summary • Editing Overview • Hiring Editors • Peer Review Process Summary • Marketing and Communications Summary • Marketing and Communications Overview • Release Summary

		• Release Overview • Adoption Summary • Adoption Overview • Improvements and Maintenance Summary • Improvements and Maintenance Overview • Adaptations Summary • Adaptations Overview • Making Open Textbooks: A Video Guide • Feedback and Suggestions • About the Team • Accessibility Assessment • Licensing Information • Version History
	30 September 2019	Following chapters or sections edited for typos, Canadian spelling, or updated for broken links and other information: • About Rebus Community • Building a Team Overview • How to Build a Leadership Team • Recruitment Guide • Roles and Responsibilities • Managing Volunteers • Engagement Guide • Project Scoping Overview • Project Summary Template • Authoring and Content Creation Overview • Author Guide Template • Peer Review Process Guide • Review Guide Template (Google Docs) • Review Guide Template Hypothes.is) • Review Statement Template • Other Open Textbooks Created with Rebus Community Support
	9 June 2020	Added: • [Example] Proposed Formatting Workflow • [Example] Formatting Accessible Tables
	29 September 2021	Revised: • Author Guide Template • About Rebus Community • Other Open Textbooks Created with Rebus Community Support

www.ingramcontent.com/pod-product-compliance
Lightning Source LLC
Chambersburg PA
CBHW051507050726
47594CB00010B/3998